The Song of Circe and Other Simple Musings

J. Matthew Helms

THE SONG OF CIRCE

AND OTHER SIMPLE MUSINGS

BELLE ISLE BOOKS
www.belleislebooks.com

Copyright © 2022 by J. Matthew Helms

No part of this book may be reproduced in any form or by any electronic or mechanical means, or the facilitation thereof, including information storage and retrieval systems, without permission in writing from the publisher, except in the case of brief quotations published in articles and reviews. Any educational institution wishing to photocopy part or all of the work for classroom use, or individual researchers who would like to obtain permission to reprint the work for educational purposes, should contact the publisher.

ISBN: 978-1-953021-67-0
LCCN: 2022900198

Printed in the United States of America

Published by
Belle Isle Books (an imprint of Brandylane Publishers, Inc.)
5 S. 1st Street
Richmond, Virginia 23219

BELLE ISLE BOOKS
www.belleislebooks.com

belleislebooks.com | brandylanepublishers.com

For Sharon, Shane, Aidan, and everyone else who has supported me along the way.

CONTENTS

THE SONG OF CIRCE AND THE WESTERN WANDERER

PRELUDE	3
OF DREAMS	7
THE QUEST FOR CIRCE	13
THE BREAKING OF THE DAWN	22
EPILOGUE	27

A CONTINUED COLLECTION OF WORDS

OF SIMPLE MUSINGS	30
THE HOUSE OF SADNESS	53
BLACK BIRDS AND CELESTIAL ADVERSARIES	68
THE COMPANION	75
POSTSCRIPT	96

THE LAMENT OF VICTUS

PART 1—THE EMANCIPATION OF HALCYON	98
PART 2—THE FREEING OF CASSIOPEIA	100
PART 3—FENRIR'S SACRIFICE	103
PART 4—CIRCE AND THE THREE DOORS OF TARTARUS	107
PART 5—THE MEETING OF ZEUS	117
PART 6—THE NEW DAWN	121

A LIGHT WITHIN THE NIGHTMARES

PART 1—UPON THE MEETING BY THE BIRCH	126
PART 2—OF ELVES AND MISUNDERSTANDINGS	130
PART 3—A CAVE FOR CAUCHEMAR'S CURSE	134
PART 4—THE DESTRUCTION OF PALAIS DES RÊVES	138
PART 5—THE RISING OF A KING	141
PART 6—THE CROWNING OF ALIENOR	143
PART 7—WAR	146
PART 8—THE BRAVE GIRL, THE QUEEN, THE ELF, THE SORCERER, AND THE DRAGON	150
PART 9—DEPARTING FROM PALAIS DES RÊVES	153
ABOUT THE AUTHOR	157

THE SONG OF CIRCE AND THE WESTERN WANDERER

PRELUDE

OF DREAMS

THE QUEST FOR CIRCE

THE BREAKING OF THE DAWN

EPILOGUE

PRELUDE

(1)

The mariner's star whispers to the waking crescent moon,
Asking to hear the song that's only sung in lunar tune.
Of Circe, the Dragon Queen, from the eastern meadow lands
And the softly howling wolf that fell helpless in her hands.

The crescent moon takes in a breath, preparing for her tome,
And all the stars go dim within their universal dome.
The crickets and cicadas sing to announce the coming song.
Mercury and Venus cannot help but hum along.

The night wind stops and settles down to find itself a seat,
And the trees hush noisy rivers so that all can hear the suite.
The clouds huddle in silence at the base of rolling hills,
So as not to stand opposing all the eager daffodils.

And all about grows quiet, becoming lost in the lunar muse
As she paints bright the night with her wonderous storied hues.
The song of forbidden fate, written down since time began—
The song of Circe's taming of the great, fierce Vanargand.

(2)

What words can I write that have not yet been written
By those come before—wiser, sharper in pen?
Shall I speak incantations to summon forth a muse
Who can whisper the unknown verse I should use?

Shall I speak more of shadows, dragons, and flame
As I again curse the gods in the power of your name?
Perhaps I can wander through a desolate land
Or venture a quest for the maiden fair's hand.

Ships I will sail; on vast seas I will fly,
Searching for rhymes to make even stones cry.
Perchance I will fail and be lost to the stars;
The 'spanse of the heavens to become binding bars.

Will the demons of darkness again gather in hate
To strike from me lyrics to lift your worried state?
If, when they gather, you're in need of a song,
I pray those words to come swiftly and spring true and long.

For I fear not the night and its tenants of black,
Nor do I shake when the clouds send lighting to crack.
I choose not to enter this contest of violence,
But I will take up arms against fear of mute silence.

(3)

Here lies a tale of two beset in naught but simple words.
Of the one, he is but a common western wanderer;
And of her, possessing a radiance unmatched by all else;
Who were perchance to meet in spite of distant, foreign shores.

They met in a place along the riverside
And chose then to venture off into trueness and light.
For each other, they brought forth smiles and laughter on darker days.
Though they knew time was short, they ran together as one.

He sang her songs joyous and new, seeking only to bring a smile.
She filled his heart and so ignited his pen to flow.
He sought to find her the morning and night each day.
From across the seas, she gave her hand and brought him up above.

Ever in a field of tulips shall the goddess sit,
calling forth the sunrise on the rolling eastern hills,
casting light then forth across the tempestuous seas,
lighting the mind and heart of the common western wanderer.

(4)

A lone wolf shuffles in the black before dawn.
Though hungry and gaunt, he hunts not for the fawn.
He gathers up bones before the breaking of light
As he makes preparations for his sacred rite.

He calls forth the fires from deep in the ground
As he releases the magic that in his blood is bound.
The black hills in silence tremble then at his call,
Forces seen and unseen falling under his thrall.

His gaze fixed, resolute, across the chilling wave,
For in the east live demons he knows he must stave.
For as darkness gathers so far from his reach,
He will do all he can so the light can then breach.

So forth on a path marked by enchanted skies,
He'll focus his power in hopes of easing the cries.
And he prays they remain slumbereing all the night long
As he howls for them this simple spell of a song.

(5)

In the west beyond the shores,
There is a desolate tract
Of dust and stone, upon which
A steel fence stands intact.

But in this land of bones and death
And biting wind throughout,
There grows now a single rose,
Bright and strong and stout.

In the east across the seas,
There spreads a field of green,
And in this lush and wondrous land,
A single tulip there is seen.

Its bright and radiant glow does shine,
Casting all within its glorious light.
Its mere existence calls 'cross the sea
And brings the western rose to life.

Upon one another do they stare,
Yearning to grow in the same fertile ground.
But the sea is vast, and the storms are great,
So they only reply to the other's sound.

Yet as they to each other smile,
Hoping perchance they shall embrace.
To cross the sea and meet as one,
hand to hand and face to face.

OF DREAMS

(1)

Sleep now. Sleep to dream, as in dreams we are free.
Free from burdens, free from strife. Free to hope and free to run.
So sleep now, my muse and my queen.
Sleep and dream and be free.

Do I dream? For this cannot be real.
The stars cry out, and the seas give praise.
The muse of the heavens shines forth again,
And the smile of my soul is seen once more.

The spark of hope.
The spread of fire from her rubied lips.
The gaze of peace from her enchanting eyes.
The heavens grow envious at the song of her voice.

She drifts into slumber so far from my arms,
Needing no guard to watch for threat.
I call out from the shore across the sea so vast.
Goodnight, my queen; my fair Circe.

(2)

Wake not to fear, nor to worry,
For I have not left you as it seems.
Look out west, where the sun doth point,
For there I stand, across the seas.

Neither the horses of Helios
Nor any wild beasts of Hades
Have the strength bestowed upon them
To keep me from returning.

So as the morning light dawns
And the world stirs to wake,
Look not afar, sweet maiden fair,
For there I stand, your fair-worded fool.

(3)

Fall not upon the softest cloud,
Or upon a pillow of wind.
Yet I beg of you, my dear Circe,
Fall here, into my arms.

For this night is long, cold, and dark,
And many a beast tarries about.
But I shall protect you, my dear Circe,
Right here in my arms.

So sleep, and sleep well,
For this night you are safe—
Safe from all worry, my queen Circe,
Right here in my arms.

I wonder what a goddess dreams
When she lays her head to rest.
Does she dream of mountaintops
Or of the endless skies?

Will she see a rolling brook,
Singing soft and sweet and low?
Does she see the watching wolf
Ever standing as her guard?

Does she spend the night
Dancing amongst the stars,
Resting briefly as she flies
To sit atop the moon?

Will she dream of tulips
As far as can be seen,
Stippled soft, standing still,
Moving only in the breeze?

Dare I be so bold and muse
And arrogantly suppose
That in her dreams she sees herself also,
Right here in my arms?

(4)

I gaze once more as you begin to drift,
Sailing off across the sea.
I hold back tears and stand yet firm
Watching as you fly away.

It is only the night, the blink of an eye,
But long this night pulls me so.
I find your eyes and paint them here
On my heart to carry me through.

Do me this kindness and dream of me.
For as I dream, I dream always of you.
And if, by chance, be it in heaven or hell,
Perhaps we shall meet as we both do dream.

(5)

Circe sits sleepily, shadowed in the shade
While the wolf walks willfully in wonderment of her ways,
Peacefully padding, politely pawing, passing to her place,
With lilting laughter, looking longingly whilst lying in her lap,
Both basking blissfully beneath the branches of the birch,
Happily holding hands here for however long they have.

(6)

Lay down your weary head, and do so not in fear.
For tonight I plead to the gods so the many all may hear:
Let her rest now softly, and but dream the sweetest dreams.
Stitch together the restful hours in smooth, unrendable seams.

Keep her warm as the north wind blows and chills this winter night.
May she be greeted by eastern glow as her day's first sight.
Please, oh gods, grant my call and meet it with no guile!
Give her the peace that brings about only her perfect smile!

But if she should wake kindly, whisper softly in her ear
That although her "there" is so distant from my "here,"
In the sky she'll see each shining light of moon and star.
Thus overall, our miles apart are really not that far.

(7)

I stand in armor on the shores of your dreams,
Guarding your peace by all possible means,
Armed and prepared for what may stalk and creep,
With a torch raised high to guard your soft sleep.

I will break the chains and scorch the briars,
Battle the dragons and drink their fires.
Nothing shall pass betwixt mineself and thine.
For your comfort, I'll ever hold to this line.

And once the storm is passed and through,
I'll lay you down in fields anew.
Sleep again, oh my maiden fair;
Sleep softly again, and without care.

For in your dreams, I am ever near
To chase away all you may fear.
My face you'll see in the soft moonlight
With my arms around you every night.

(8)

Dream not of worries and dream not of cares.
Dream not of tomorrow or the burdens that stare.
Dream of the dawn in which there is no sea,
And if it be to your aid, please dream of me.

We've cast the spells that hide in your eyes
And opened the doors behind which magic lies.
I've set the sails into the fair-blowing breeze;
We make for the pass through the thick South Downs trees.

I will steer our ship around every brewing storm
And strike down all who would attack us with scorn.
I am here in the stars to ease your every trial.
So lay down your head and sleep with a smile.

Let us bask in this realm where the magic is real
And hold tight to the joy that we each do feel.
For the oceans are smaller when we meet in dreams,
As narrow as the last of the River Wey's streams.

(9)

In quiet, still hours when Night herself is at rest,
The only things stirring are the clouds in the west,
Which coax from their slumber a gentle, warm breeze
To sing softly through branches of leaf-barren trees.

Their song cleanses the air of past days' blight
And ushers in dreams of laughter and light.
As the moon looks down, giving its smiling glow,
The streams in turn glimmer with thanks as they flow.

So in her chamber, Circe sleeps sound through the eve
As the world all about brings its own thread to weave,
Crafting its comfort solely for its queen's sleep,
To ensure she falls softly, pleasant, and deep.

For in this hour of night, there is no call for greetings
As one sleeps, such that words call for no replied meetings.
This song sent from Vanargand on the tail of a star,
Reminding fair Circe he is not but so far.

THE QUEST FOR CIRCE

(1)

She waits with open arms in the furthest corner of the crescent moon.
I wish to call her from the garden below and beckon her to me soon.

Shall I sing a song to charm her and swing her heavenly eyes?
Or proclaim the way of all there is in an effort to seem wise?

I move to speak and call her name, but words then fail my lips.
Panicked tears fall from my eyes; I fall to fear's cold grips.

But to my side she flies and floats with intoxicating grace.
All treasures found throughout the earth compare not to her face.

Her hands hold every star, to be hung high within the 'spanse,
And she takes me by my shaking hand and offers me to dance.

Wake me not if this beautiful dance be but a passing dream!
Let me bask in warming light that doth from her presence beam!

For I wish to live in here now, ever fixed within her gaze—
dancing through the night with her for all my remaining days!

(2)

Circe sits with tears in her eyes,
Looking down from her windowsill.
The wolf paces in the court below,
Howling softly in the long night's chill.

He sees her clearly as she sees him,
Close enough to feel but too far to touch.
He calls to her daily, nightly, and more,
Her attention and presence never too much.

The wolf looks upon her with care and concern.
She says she is well and never to worry.
But as he paces, he sees her, knowing
Her tears and words tell a different story.

The court a chasm, the wall an ocean,
He longs to hold her and be her protection.
But as it is, he does all he is able
And howls his song of undying affection.

(3)

A fool sits upon the sand,
Speaking his words into the breeze.
Will the wind be kind and carry them on
Across the sea to the maiden fair?

A fool stands upon the shore,
Shouting his soul toward the waves.
Will the tides be kind and carry them on
Across the sea to the maiden fair?

A fool falls upon his knees,
Pleading his desire to the sky above.
Will the stars be kind and sing his song
Across the sea to the maiden fair?

A fool charges into the sea,
Caring not for what lies ahead.
Damn the wind, the tides, and stars,
For he shall cross to the maiden fair!

(4)

Circe stands in all her glory,
Shrouded in mist of darkness and light.
I fall before her, rapt and weak,
Exposed and bare, putting up no fight.

Circe smiles and reaches down,
Her eyes giving courage, her hair shining bright.
I stand before her, feigning strength,
Clothed in her smile, made by her sight.

Circe sits on a horse cut from glass,
Taking me up to ride far from the night.
I cling to her flesh as we ride 'cross the sea,
Equally entranced by her beauty and might.

Circe lies on the shores of my mind.
I stand watch and guard from wolves and their bite.
She breaks the chains and unlocks the gates,
And I ever will strive to keep her safe from all fright.

(5)

I woke in the night, frightened and cold,
Fearing you'd left without a word told.
So I rose in that hour, blinded with tears,
Seeking the maiden who could calm my fears.

Coat on my back and staff in my hand,
I set out across this desolate land,
Burning the bridges as each one I crossed,
Not slowing from wind or from biting frost.

I came to the mountains, blocking my way—
Sheer cliffs of granite, tall, cold, and gray.
They stood with pride and without care,
But crumbled when I named the maiden fair.

Passing through valleys overcome with shadow,
Over dried brooks where streams no longer flow,
I forged ever onward in my heart's great quest,
Ever into the east, looking not to the west.

The forest was heavy, no light could break.
So I tread through the darkness for my own heart's sake.
The pines watched and mocked me, lost in their lair,
But parted when I named the maiden fair.

Farther I ran, o'er thorn, stick, and stone.
The light of her eyes through the long night shone.
Her face, inspiration; her sweet voice my song,
I'll smite beast and man to be where I belong.

The shore rose before me, the waves making threat.
But in spite of its wrath, I turned back not yet.
I laughed at the tides and cursed at the spray,
Knowing I still walked the righteous way.

The thunderous crash and malicious reach—
I would not be moved from the sands of this beach.
When I fell to my knees and cried aloud to the air,
The seas parted at the name of the maiden fair.

Her song growing louder, her light shining brighter,
I now reach eastern shores, my resolve never tighter.
I cross through field and over rolling hill,
No shadow darkening my desire or will.

My feet ever constant, my heart finds the way.
She guides me to her as the dawn guides the day.
At the gate, the wolf greets me with a welcoming stare
As I whisper to it the name of my maiden fair.

Across the court and at last through the door,
I can fall at her feet, searching no more.
Another step my legs can no longer bear,
As I fall into the arms of my beautiful maiden fair.

(6)

I cast a stone into the ocean, calling out to speak a word.
But in reply, the wordless shouts of hungry gulls
And the waves in their abuse upon the shore was all I heard.

I cast another stone therein and cursed Poseidon's name,
Supposing then the bastard may rise and speak for but a time,
But as I watched and my rage still grew, the old god never came.

I cast a coin into the sea and knelt in reverent pause.
I pleaded with the god to grant me just one simple wish,
But in spite of all my fervent prayers, he ne'er did heed my cause.

So I turned my back upon the waters and their lesser god,
Cast aside all my allegiance and faith that once was,
Decided and determined Poseidon is naught but a fraud.

This ocean that stands between you and I taunts us even still.
So I called upon the goddess of the green and fertile land.
If Poseidon will not answer me, perhaps then Gaia will.

May the goddess of the pastures green grant a moment spare
And cast a bridge across the sea to spite that weaker god.
Allow me even the briefest time to hold my maiden fair.

But even Gaia does not stir when I call my plea to her,
The only answer in my ear the empty, hollow wind.
So I'll be as cast and don the cloak of a simple wretched cur.

I'll fell the trees and by my hands I'll make the long boards join,
Weaving the wheat as an amber sail and hoist upon the mast.
I'll sail across Poseidon's court on a ship of Gaia's coin.

I fear you not, so throw your tempests and shake apart your land.
Call forth the waves and spray, and monsters of the deep.
For tall, determined, marching forth are the legs on which I stand.

I will sail to you across this empty, vast, aquatic space,
Laughing in the faces of the worthless, silent gods.
For no ocean, land, or beast should stop us meeting face to face.

(7)

Take flight! Climb the wind and to my arms fly,
For in this world of ours that we create,
The laws, bonds, and shackles shall not apply.

The oceans are small if we do so believe;
The sun, ever warm, still does shine in the rain,
The breath of your laugh the only wind in the trees.

We can walk together beneath the sea
And hold the stars within our palms.
We wake the night simply to set it free.

We will call forth dragons and mighty gales,
No chains or stones standing in our path
As we float 'cross the moon upon golden sails.

As king and queen over all that exists,
We have no cages, no walls or gates.
I'll grant everything your heart ever wished.

So fly now to me as I paint the sky blue.
We'll meet in the air, naming the winds,
For here in this world, there is but I and you.

(8)

For Circe does Vanargand keep a watchful eye about,
On guard should he ever hear her give a cry or shout.
Prepared to battle man or beast that should ever dare intrude,
Or settle at her feet with hope to ease unsettled mood.

She granted him his life at the dark breaking of December.
The days before then, he finds not worthy to remember.
For great Vanargand wants not to return to the night
When he finds such peace in basking in Circe's warm light.

For in the narrow corner between Valhalla and Atlantis,
They have forged a realm together where only they exist.
A land of ships that sail across an endless sea of stars,
Where they need not walk in fear of their pasts or of their scars.

The great Wolf and the Goddess who ought never to have met
But found each other, regardless of the borders fate had set.
As they steer across oceans and stone paths to tread,
They return in their longing to journey together ahead.

(9)

In haste and hurry Vanargand runs across the mythic plains,
Breaking walls and rules without care for fictional chains.
He leaps high over Kattegat, streaking forth from his halls.
He steps across Anholt to splash through Nervion's falls.

Turning east, he bounds along Mediterranean tides,
Setting forth for the land where fair Circe resides,
From Valhalla to Atlantis, 'cross the wide expanse,
His heart seeking deep magic in her gaze that enchants.

He climbs Olympus with furious and thunderous power
As gods, fae, nymphs, and peasants before his might cower.
He calls forth for Circe to steal from Helios' halls,
And together they build a palace where there exist no walls.

They plant the new Glasir in the Arcadia they create,
Resolute none but they shall henceforth decide their fate.
So in spite of wide seas and celestial separation,
They'll share their days, no mind the risk of their deities' damnation.

(10)

I must apologize for my failure this night,
For as the moon rose, I was too weary to write.
The words would not gather as they oft did before.
I fear your opinion of me now be turned sore.

Please be not angry, nor look on me with scorn,
Like one promised tulips but instead given thorns.
My intentions are constant, have been all these days long,
Naught more but to give you a smile from a song.

Oh, to sing of your radiant, infinite grace
Or the warmth that I feel from the sight of your face.
Your voice from the heavens that speaks words so wise;
No volumes yet writ convey the allure of your eyes.

I wish to find the words as they dance on the wind
And pray this draught of lexeme soon will rescind.
So here I plead to you, tender-hearted Circe:
Grant this night your Vanargand his unearned mercy.

THE BREAKING OF THE DAWN

(1)

The night is broken from the east,
But light shines not from the stars.
A frost grips the world around me,
Yet my eyes open to comforting warmth.

A call that breaks my sleeping dreams
And guides my ships across the seas.
A light that glows in emerald green,
Her name unspoken, her face hidden.

The song of her voice awakens me now;
Her spirit unlocks my secret desire.
She holds my hand and shows the way,
A siren sent from the shores of afar.

The night is broken from the east,
But light shines not from the stars.
A frost grips the world around me,
Yet my eyes open to comforting warmth.

(2)

Break! Break, you bastard light!
This darkness hangs heavy
As the moon laughs with spite.

Where, oh where is my new dawn?
I pace through the sand
As the waves taunt me with song.

"Lux!" I cry, and curse, and swear.
The beastly night knows well my want:
I wish only to look on the maiden fair.

(3)

The darkness returns in her well-worn thread,
But my greeting for her is no longer in dread.
Tarry away, be far from me this night,
For in the east gathers the emerald light.

Cast then your storms and scorch then my land,
My feet shan't be moved, not by beast or by hand.
And you I'll grant nothing, not breath and not sight,
For in the east gathers the emerald light.

I no longer hold fear of the darkness that lurks
Or worry myself over her masterworks.
My soul has found reason to soar high in flight,
For in the east gathers the emerald light.

(4)

Look for me when first you wake,
When the dawn cowers at your sight.
Weeping as it does so long,
Calling mists to hide its light.

I shall wage war on all that harm,
Setting our light in fields of green,
And casting the beasts that snarl and bite
Back into their dark lairs unseen.

The dusk will come and threaten our day;
The moon will laugh its boasting glow.
But on the shores of purple night,
Hand in hand, forward we go.

I'll guide our ships through every storm
And melancholy when life is tilt;
I'll wipe your tears and hold you close,
For nothing can break what we have built.

(5)

Rise! Rise, oh Goddess, and claim this day!
For as the dawn conquers the east,
So shall this day be yours!
Fear not yesterday's folly!
Think not of its troubles,
For you rise!
Rise as the swelling tide
Lifting the largest ships!
Rise as the mountains
Lifting the clouds!
Stand as the oaks,
Unshakeable and strong!
Stretch your branches high,
As nothing shall move you!
Rise, oh Goddess, and rule this day!
Rise!

(6)

The half-moon fades in the western sky.
As Helios calls forth the eastern dawn,
Circe rises to name the day.

From her hallowed slumber she doth rise,
And standing tall in the naked light,
Circe rises to claim the day.

She walks forth with power and grace
As mountains tremble and rivers halt;
Circe rises to conquer the day.

Clothed in clouds, announced by the winds.
All fall before her in humble reverence.
Circe rises to defeat the day.

God and Goddess avert their eyes.
They cower in fear before her path.
Circe rises, and all fall before her.

(7)

The stars shine brighter when the moon is off to hide,
With naught as reminder save the weeping tide.
Simply look to Ursa and her matronly stare,
For as she is in the sky, so too am I there.

The stars shine brighter when the moon is dressed in black,
Taunting the seas as if it may never come back.
But Orion the hunter will bear the task at hand
And guide passage to the sailor of the far-off sand.

The stars shine brighter when the moon is asleep,
Enchanted by secrets it still fights to keep.
Fix your chariot to Taurus, mighty and strong,
For whom no burden's too great nor journey too long.

The stars shine brighter when the moon is being coy,
Hiding with mischief like the soldiers at Troy.
But soon the sun will waken like a gentle fawn,
And the stars will take their bow to usher forth the dawn.

EPILOGUE

(1)

Let me pull the canvas yet again, fair maiden of the eastern shore,
Sailing back to when I would bid you goodnight in the days gone long before,
When the stars would guide us through the night's most treacherous seas
And my only purpose with these words was to put your mind at ease.

Do you recall the quiet sound as the ship cut through life's many waves?
Recounting the many demons that your kind regard did serve to stave:
All the journeys of fierce Vanargand and the kindly goddess of green light
And how the Viking wolf was but an un-whelped pup within her sight.

Shall I curse the many gods again to reclaim my place once held,
Fighting to release your splendid glory, as it swelled?
Poseidon, Gaia, Helios, and Zeus, all bastards by their name;
In spite of all the storms, they could never douse your burning flame.

So on this winter night wherein the mists come gather yet again,
Look once more for your western fool, at the gates where dreams begin.
With his open hand to guide you to the peace dreams should always be,
Greeting the goddess Circe with reverence upon his bended knee.

So if only for this night once more, before the light doth crest,
Let Vanargand be yours tonight and do what he does at his best:
Stand and watch for you as you venture into the stars' expanse,
Where, upon the gold grains of the moon, with you he waits to dance.

(2)

The closing of the chapter, the end of the tale.
As the sun rises here, in the west it must fail.
So think not of trouble and think not of pain.
Think not of the wolf and think not of blame.

For Circe must rise, with her proud head held high,
And sooner or later, the wolf must flee from her side.
Remember to laugh if you think of his face,
And be quick to smile at metaphorical embrace.

Nothing of that which has been said to you
Should ever be thought of or found as untrue.
Whether read in metered and rhythmic time
Or read aloud poorly in crude slant rhyme.

As a ship sails off to Poseidon's own land,
The sails growing smaller than white grains of sand
Know their time here was blissful, joyous, and sweet,
Ever grateful that they had the fortune to meet.

So rise, great goddess, and claim now your throne,
And forget not the light that you have shone
As a wolf sits upon distant rocks of the west,
Knowing his time with you was ever the best.

Promise him this, and this as a last:
That you'll never discard the ventured past.
Remember this now, and perhaps yet again,
So that Circe can live, even now . . . even then.

A CONTINUED
COLLECTION OF WORDS

OF SIMPLE MUSINGS

THE HOUSE OF SADNESS

BLACK BIRDS AND
CELESTIAL ADVERSARIES

THE COMPANION

POSTSCRIPT

OF SIMPLE MUSINGS

(1)

I kneel by the smoldering remnant with a prayer on my lips.
I fan gently, pleading to see the glow return once more—
The warmth a near memory as the last of the smoke ascends,
For as the flame has flown away, it is but the embers that remain.

I cherish now these glowing pieces and all that they mean.
As the amber hues move and crawl, I see your face even still.
But December turned cold and gray with a chilling, cruel wind
And so the fire burned low, and only the embers still remain.

So by my hand and hopeful determination, I will sit and I will watch,
Tears constantly pressing my eyes like dogs loosed on a hunt,
Blowing ever so lightly to see pulsing life briefly again rise.
But in spite of my pleas, only the embers remain.

I fear the darkness that I know looms ever so close behind.
What light is left before me is my only source of comfort now.
I wince at the growing gray, and I curse at the cooling ashes.
I know our time is short and fleeting, as only the embers remain.

(2)

Two trains passing through the night
As they traverse through the Pyrenees.
The mountains' silhouette against the sky
Decorated by swaying Spanish trees.

Passing as they thunder silently by
The hollowed-out prints of the mountain feet.
Such that none aboard take time to view
The wonderment of their fateful meet.

The meeting here in this time and place
Of all possible points that rise and fade.
In all the moments that have passed
And those still called as debts unpaid.

Do they think of the paths that lead them on
Here as they glance across the way?
The moments of happenstance unfolded,
Each turn they made throughout the day?

Each one yearning from their quiet corner
For a far-off place to find their being.
From valleyed crossroads now they fly
Without a glance to see who else is dreaming:

Some for tales of ancient Valladolid,
To seek what secrets she might share.
While others dream of softer shores
Found only in Saintes Maries de la Mer.

Do they see their fellow travelers as
They stream and fade through formless gray?
Or are we each a faceless train
That speeds off, going the wrong way?

(3)

The maple in the park stands tall and strong
As the March wind passes to sing its song.
New life springs forth in budding green
As winter slips off to slumber and dream.

The maple in the park spreads wide its arms,
Shading all from the summer sun's harm—
A place of repose for the tired and weak,
Ever ready to shelter all who would seek.

The maple in the park is robed in splendor—
An autumn display of red, yellow, amber.
Fearing not in its want to be ever so bold,
It throws a spectacle of color for all to behold.

The maple in the park lays bare in December,
Its beauty once held such that none can remember.
And all who were sheltered now hurry down the street,
Quick to crush its once prized leaves under feet.

(4)

The stones break forth in the falling tide,
Showing the secrets they chose to hide
With colorful shouts on their gray façade,
To prove that perception is often flawed.

The genteel recession of the river's hand
Shows life that's found beneath desolate land.
In cold gray December I was given a gift
That just for a moment a heavy mind did lift.

So, stopping and staring, to marvel at this:
That even in darkness, one may find bliss.
Knowing that ever when the tides so return,
Beneath the black waters, a vibrance does burn.

So turning away to leave now this found wonder,
I watch as the tide swells up from down under.
And in knowing it being soon once more unseen,
One cannot help but recall the secret garden of green.

(5)

I find beauty in the broken pieces.
The jagged edges cut my skin, pulling you into my veins,
Consuming my thoughts like bleeding ink as it spreads and stains.
I pray the high never ceases.

I see poetry in the mess.
The structured dysfunction shatters on the bordering line,
Spilling over like the edge of what walls would confine.
I hope the chaos to never regress.

I see sculpture in the flame.
The consumption as smoke billows, filling the air;
The sting of the heat and the blinding glare—
A desire that will not tame.

I see freedom in destruction:
The foundations of bridges from the ash of burnt cages;
The formless shapes of aimless lines etched across blank pages—
Because templates are the obstruction.

(6)

I returned to visit with a dear old friend,
Though my life began well after he met his end.
He speaks few words and won't tell me his name,
Or how long he's watched, or from whence he came.

His weathered, worn face and haggard lines
Speak through the stories he tries to hide.
I read of the storms he has well withheld
And see the times death's attempts were felled.

I ask many questions, all answered with silence,
But nothing hides his years of stubborn defiance.
So we sit, and I talk, and I count all his scars
As we both watch and wait for the soon-coming stars.

The river his court and the rocks as his jesters,
Common folk like myself stop by just to pester.
This king who was planted here by floods and storms,
Like an oak that sits watching as the wide world transforms.

As the time of our parting came for this day,
I quietly thanked him before turning away.
The sun beating down and the river receding,
I gave a grateful nod to all his years preceding.

(7)

I know now what must be done.
Cut the anchor; let the ship run.
Smash the sextant and sail by feel.
Create the world you wish were real.

The safety nets now cast aside,
The time has come to freely ride,
No ropes or catch to hold within.
Fall into what must now begin.

Old Valhalla fades into the clouds;
A blazing new dawn burns off the shrouds.
Ignore the knucklebones toward you cast
And plunge the blade into the past.

The road to here matters not for there,
So grasp the wind and hold the air.
Ever forward, never admitting defeat,
Shaping the sounds of your own journey's suite.

(8)

Bloodstained cobbles cry out at the statue's feet.
Our symbols of oppression adorn this historic street.
Granite and bronze memorialize our old, egregious sins—
Perpetuate a system where progress never quite begins.

Stars and bars with red hats, flying twisted southern crosses,
While we count the old fight won and ignore our modern losses.
Children dying at the hand of the badged protector—
Our justice system looming like a great white-sheeted specter.

The inward-looking, whitewashed walls of selfish self-denials
Turning stubbornly blind eyes to the many scale-tipped trials.
But it goes beyond the rhetoric shouted down from Capitol Hill,
Because in this neo-Crow system, emancipation's waiting still.

Freedoms still denied for those who live outside the mold
Because of skin tone, language, or the god and faith they hold.
What will it take to make the weak excuses finally halt
And understand we all hold part of our ancestral fault?

So how do we make the changes that we know are sorely needed?
How do I ensure my children always stand by those unfairly treated?
How to teach them hate and prejudice are more than simple words
And to foster conversations in which those who must be are heard?

The key to growing past our past will go beyond just talking
If we are to understand the paths our neighbors still are walking.
White America must be the first to change the legacy
And admit this fight won't end till we destroy supremacy.

(9)

As flies are found in swarms wherever flesh has turned to rot
And ashes are the only signs of what once burned bright and hot,
Blood and bones continue to fund the vicious red empire
As complacency absorbs our lives like a silent vampire.

As the lush islands of infinite shores burn before our eyes,
Smoke blotting out the sun in plumes as it continues still to rise,
The backyard of our planet screams aloud in fiery pain
While our leaders elsewhere make sure only innocence is slain.

As history at its apogee makes once more to reset
With neo-fascism parading, a woolen white-clothed threat,
Designing novel wars to keep his power from decreasing,
Indifferent to the fires, our planet, or countless lives deceasing.

Is this world like a bridge that cannot reach the other side?
A ship that has been built only to sink in the rising tide?
Remains of shattered glass that once were held so close and dear,
Broken by the foolishness that rang so loud and clear.

If in religion is compassion, as is so widely claimed to be,
Then what sense can be found in the broken world I see?
Are a privileged few set with such grand, remarkable uses
While others are built only for constant struggle and abuses?

(10)

The last light fades along the western horizon's bleak façade,
And with it comes the torment of another lonely night to trod.
But nothing of this cold, bitter world is found to be so tragic
That it cannot be remedied either with matches or with magic.

The twilight dons its nightly black attire as it mourns,
For Henry is always Edward no matter which face he adorns.
And no threat is found down in the streets so violently graphic
That it cannot be remedied either with matches or with magic.

The moon shines out a weak attempt to thwart each kind of beast,
Trying to reflect the glimmering that calls out from the east.
As the pale light battles darkness, it is never so erratic
That it cannot be remedied either with matches or with magic.

As the cold night nears the end of its long, dark, lonely path,
And the battle has been fought with such vigor, fury, and wrath,
It should never be considered then a measure far too drastic
That it cannot be remedied either with matches or with magic.

(11)

Many words I've written, and some tales I've even told,
But I confess within them, there is no moral to behold.
I'll never be so bold as to think I could reshape the earth
Or place upon myself more value than I am truly worth.

I say this not for sorrow or to coax pity from your eyes
But to speak with perfect candor without vanity or guise.
For while the road I've trod in life has been narrow and quite plain,
I'll gladly share what few conclusions my foolish musings sometimes gain:

Do not mistake the demons that prey on your darker hours
As anything but bastards who work to topple your strong towers.
Confuse them not with fallen angels who tarry still about,
Condemned for choosing to pursue unknown truths in days of doubt.

For what is right and what is wrong when numbered few are our days?
The world is not made of black and white or the varied tones of grays.
The moments that make you stop and smile are those to be pursued.
Embrace the colors that swallow the gray, so vibrant and hued.

The sun will rise, the earth will spin, as it has done before,
Caring not for those who roam upon mountain or on shore.
So find the places in these days that fill your eyes with light,
And listen not to bitter mice pontificating wrong and right.

I've seen the brilliant radiance that shines within your soul
And felt the way your simplest words can piece one back to whole.
Light the fires that deep inside you still ache to brightly burn,
And drink the tears of fools who stand opposing like smooth Sauternes.

One life we are given, and to this we are charged as such:
"Do what is right, not what is wrong; this is little, this is much."
Who are these foreign, fabled gods to build such cages and walls?
Never fear to follow your heart to wherever the wind so calls.

(12)

To Aegir's house I now return to humbly confess
To how I did by word and deed against his might transgress:
Speaking ill of his great halls and of his liquid kingdom;
Taking for granted that he holds the only keys to freedom.

For I long to be immersed within his realm once more,
To go out beyond the Jorth and her long, sand-dressed shore.
Baptize this sinner once again, oh great god of the sea.
Let your fists of might and salt again upon me be!

So grant me passage, this I beg, oh merciful sea lord.
Let me pass beyond your gates that I may be restored.
Please lend to me a kindly ear and a soft heart as I plead,
For I have but little of that which from your waters I need.

So I close my eyes and smell the salt carried on the wind,
Enveloped in the mist that makes all darkness rescind.
The essence of the love that you and your queen, Rán, do share
Fills my lungs to cleanse away all worry and all care.

I stand here now upon the shore, appealing to your daughters.
I hold my breath a moment more before trespassing your waters.
Dancing along the water's edge, they call to beckon in;
Cold hands to steal my breath away as they grasp my skin.

These waves crash overtop my head, embracing now my all.
They push and pull me with the tide, but never let me fall.
They lift me higher as I float, now safe within their hands,
Floating freely, needing not my feet upon the sands.

With a clear, encouraging song, they lead me farther still,
For Aegir and his consort, Rán, are of mercy and goodwill.
Together now they take me in and lay me in their arms
And lower me beneath the waves where naught can do me harm.

Silence fills my eager ears like thunderous drums of peace.
The parade of endless voices now here is made to cease.
With faith restored I plant my feet, determined to do right
And spring up from the bottom to burst into the light.

I burst into the brilliant sun with all my sins behind,
Knowing new hope and strength are here, waiting for me to find.
I gasp and fill my lungs with air, new and bright and clean,
And give undying thanks below to Aegir and his queen.

(13)

Down into the sticks and leaves, the spark, still glowing, crawls,
Twisting through the kindling as old magic once more calls.
The smoke begins to whisper in announcement of the flame,
A crescendo of bright embers as I call the fire by name.

Freyja's open eye ignites in a glowing, burning light
To depose the great, vast darkness that still harbors shadowed night.
I harvest the many stars above and reap the fields of the moon
And offer my blood for safe passage, lest Hecate impugn.

The Song of Circe and Other Simple Musings

I call out to the witches who keep their practices unknown
And beckon hence unto the fields of fire Surt has sewn.
Hel and Hades soon will consummate now they've unholy wed
As Zeus and Odin sleep, ignorant, in their blinded bed.

Baldur lies there, bleeding out as Erebus and Achlys laugh,
Their cackles ringing in the night his eternal epitaph.
Atlantis soon will plummet, and Ragnarok will so rise,
Drowning mortal sorrows as it burns the gods' uncounted lies.

Circe gives a seductive smile as Fenrir growls low.
Gates are toppled as the broken souls' courage does grow.
Jupiter ascends in red to mark the final, impending doom
As roseless thorns sprout from barren, dry dirt in black bloom.

I kneel down by the burning pile of dried-out twigs and leaves.
The fire shows what will become of these deitial thieves.
In the glow of flame a smile spreads across my wicked eyes,
For from spark rises fire, drawing forth the anguished cries.

(14)

Lucifer and I met today at the park bench beside the lake
As mist hung low over the water in the cold morning's wake.
We sat quietly as the birds called out in their lyrical song,
Whilst the morning sun quietly moved the idle clouds along.

Lucifer broke the silence with a simple, small hello,
And soon therein the wisdom broke forth and began to flow.
Well-mannered and eloquent with soft-spoken, soothing speech,
She told of secrets such my mind would never solely reach.

Words that slowly cut my dogma like a two-edged blade,
Deconstructing paradigms as my beliefs began to fade.
She smiled and gazed upon my face with piercing eyes of red,
Knowing I was fully wrapped in all that She had said.

I inquired of the evils found all across the earth.
She then simply shone a light on compassion's glaring dearth.
Lucifer made the careful point that what many name as "sin"
Was first claimed to be by they who think themselves righteous within.

I mused aloud to Her upon the title "Prince of Lies."
"Men fear naught more than a wise woman with strength that defies.
For men desire power, and all beneath their heel to fall.
So Lucifer was thus penned down as male for one and all."

She told me there exists no war between Herself and the Lord
And that from the first dawn they've had a peaceable accord.
The holy men within their churches of cast brick and hewn stone
Are the fictitious writers of all the fables now well known.

I asked Her why She chose me to rend these secrets from their mask.
She playfully replied it was because I chose to ask.
Before She could depart, I asked but little more from Her lips—
Some wisdom to hold with me should my faith once more slip.

She smiled with Her eyes and turned Her soft, beautiful face,
And with the truest final words, She rose with such a grace.
"One needs not a bible to show kindness to the weak."
And saying so, She parted with a kiss upon my cheek.

(15)

The dawn breaks heavy and cold on this January morning
As first light enters like war drums in devastating warning.
But the dragon of the hills awakes not from her peaceful slumber,
As she is not the kind to be alarmed by simple thunder.

Her scales of shimmering, emerald green, her eyes of heavy black,
She fears not any mortals, nor their futile planned attack.
So many have led armies forth on bloody, murderous campaigns,
Yet here she lies upon her bed of their skeletal remains.

So she sleeps, not caring what may soon darken her door,
be it unlucky, weary traveler or foolish effort at valor.
For what can ever oppose her as she stands tall in her prime,
save the unyielding turning of the beastly hands of time?

(16)

Dear sister, dear sister,
Fret not a drop for this fool's wearisome wandering.
I simply seek shelter for mystical conjuring.
Dear sister, dear sister,
Waste not of your spirit for me to venture and find.
I've simply sauntered off and become lost within my mind.

Dear brother, dear brother,
Regale me not with your sermons of worldly science,
For what I do, I do not out of ignorance or defiance.

Dear brother, dear brother,
It is but for lack of a safe place where I can lay my head,
So I created in these dreams a new universe instead.

Dear cousin, dear cousin,
Carry word of safety to those of my kinship name.
Tell them it is only I who bears the mark of shame.
Dear cousin, dear cousin,
You're ever so welcome if you care to with me join.
Burden yourself no valise and carry you no coin.

Dear ally, dear ally,
The river wakes with fury and cries out a new song,
And I must travel to new lands where my soul does belong.
Dear ally, dear ally,
Where dragons still roam across the skies and hide up in the trees,
And the moon at night swings low to make love to the mighty seas.

Dear kindred, dear kindred,
If ever we should meet together on the shore,
Let us harvest the stars upon the ocean's vast floor.
Dear kindred, dear kindred,
We'll burn the bridge we trod just to fly in the air
As we stay lost within our minds such that none can find us there.

(17)

Fragments of bone and a single strand of your hair.
Splinters of fallen elm and jarred mist from the air.
Fire burning hot, cutting the darkness of the night.
An unkindness of ravens bringing death in their flight,
Whispering black words in the cold blowing of the breeze
And putting all companions of the foul at sinful ease.

Slaughter the calf and let the blood soak into the ground,
Calling dead to rise again in deafening, silent sound.
The earth splits as rotten dirt gives birth to fallen bones
As wolves cry to announce the terror with harrowing tones.
Cries of torment, wailing in their blood-soaked wrath—
All is ready in the calm before the aftermath.

(18)

Tell me your nightmares, and I'll tell you mine—
The intersection where fear and suspicion combine,
A place where the mind builds walls from the light
And unlocks its doors to the creatures of night.

Open your hidden baggage and I'll open mine—
A roadmap of each wrong turn and missed warning sign.
But with each sordid piece from the long-wilted past,
We can see how we have broken through every cast.

Show me your scars and I'll show you mine—
The places since healed by tears and by time,
Marks of imperfection that each tell a tale
Of succeed and survive, of misstep and fail.

(19)

Bring your guns, and I will bring my words,
For words will last longer than the bullets in your chamber.
Your pistols, your rifles, your weapons of cowardly eruption;
My stories, my philosophies, my historical understanding.

And if one of your bullets finds its way into my chest,
Somewhere in the universe, my words will still exist.
One day your blue steel will succumb to inevitable rust,
But my words will last long after my bones have turned to dust.

(20)

I fear the day the words will stop and the chain will be found broken.
When I'll take up my pen and find the stories hide, unspoken.
But until that dreaded day should break and show its demon head,
The words that drift forth from the muse above shall continue to be said.

(21)

In a rolling field of lilies where the dead come out to play,
They can laugh for a few moments before fading away.
The sunlight passes through them, but they caper even still,
Wading through the lilies and climbing every hill.

They meet as friends and meet as lovers, lost within a trance,
Taking again to one another for one final, gentle dance.
As the sun falls low, they must return again to where they're from.
And they fade into the night, eager for the next solstice to come.

(22)

Time is constant and consistent; it walks with arrogant pride.
It snaps at the heels of the moon, forcing the repetitious tide.
Laughing as the sun lies down in his remorseful drowse,
And to the hands of Time do even the stars offer their bows.

Time moves ever faster as days rapidly fall and rise,
Like fleeting glimpses flashing before my weary eyes.
Forged steel, born of fire, succumbs to eventual rust
Just as the bones of kings at the end are naught but dust.

Does one have the power to fight against the gluttonous force
Or to change direction in spite of life's predetermined course?
But Time is never thwarted, not bent to individual need,
And leaves no choice but to cut bound limbs in hope of being freed.

(23)

Inhale deeply beneath the surface where only silence exists.
Lake water fills the lungs as panic for comprehension persists.
The black water consumes the light in ways the clouds jealously dream,
Anchored by stones to the bottom, safe from the oxygenated regime.

Build new, grander castles here from the clay that lines the water's floor.
Create the place of hiding with comforts never found on shore.
A realm to rule as you see fit by wisdom, regal and hard-learned,
Where silence screams loudest, and in the dark, my solitude returned.

(24)

Standing on the peak of this valley's northern length,
Watching the river flow with slow, eternal, drumming strength,
I watch as my position never changes to grow steeper
As this relentless river cuts its way continuously deeper.

What secrets does she hide beneath her stabled surface?
Does she carry forth the stories of those with upright purpose?
Or are there tales more sinister below her genteel face,
Where naught but beast or devil reside upon this place?

I ask if she remembers the many storms of years gone past—
The ones whose rains and violence wrought her shores recast.
Does she recall the droughts of old that left her thin and frail,
Creeping slowly in the summer sun, her waters hot and stale?

I ask her of the autumn and the sentried trees on shore;
Of their sacrifice of color for the next season in store.
What of the winters, when even the bare birch branch did quiver?
Did she send forth the frigid wind simply to watch them shiver?

What does she discuss when she falls upon the sea
As they greet with warm embrace to run open and free?
I asked her all these questions, to which there was no reply.
She merely smiled knowingly as she flowed right on by.

(25)

Fear not to be tempest-minded or heavy-struck of heart,
For a faithful woman of virtue did on this day depart.
But pain will soon subside as the present becomes past,
And the joy of treasured memories will still forever last.

Though I only briefly knew her, I know this much to be true:
There can be none to question of her favoring to you.
But the pain will soon subside as the present becomes past,
And the joy of treasured memories will still forever last.

Let your tears flow freely if that be what you so need,
And let no one nor thyself count your mourning time as greed.
For the pain will soon subside as the present becomes past,
And the joy of treasured memories will still forever last.

Days will become darker, and the nights, they will be long
As you live with this new vacancy that feels unfair and wrong.
But the pain will soon subside as the present becomes past,
And the joy of treasured memories will still forever last.

(26)

Fingernails pick at the old scab to let bridled blood flow free,
Conjuring red-ribboned assurances of life that eyes can see.
I curse the calm and stillness of the water's glassy surface
As I sit in confinement by my safe, protected purchase.

Memories of chemical chaos that still bring their appeal,
Letting them run through my veins to numb all I would feel.
The relapse would be oh-so quick and done with natural ease,
Like the morphine-drip surrender to a terminal disease.

But the past chaotic rites are now locked up and stowed away
In the hope that they shall never again see the light of day.
But as visions of bottles and of pills now become as ghosts—
Demons of a new black dress descend in harmful host—

Suicidal fantasies bloom to fill the sober void,
Visions I map carefully should they ever be deployed.
I shall not make reference to them in any outspoken form,
Because my chaos is now naught but to weather the storm.

(27)

Take what you want; leave the rest behind.
Carry only the best of what you can find.
Leave twigs and stones for the next to pass
And tread only upon the soft green grass.

Take what you need and burn all that is waste.
Prove to them your threats are not made in haste.
You are the singer of whom sirens cry.
Your time of divine ruling cometh nigh.

(28)

I feel the full moon ascending to rise.
It pulls upon me like threatening tides,
Drawing me forth in the wicked rite,
Merging the black lines of hatred and spite.

Stray clouds block the light to ease coming pain
As tender flesh tears beneath the hot, pulsing strain.
The former humanity rots and then dies,
And for Ragnarok shall frightful Fenrir rise.

(29)

The fire in the corner continues to spread,
And my friends, the spiders, have long since fled.
Kindled by a cocktail of wrath and of shame,
I find that it's cold here in spite of the flame.

Pugilistic thoughts keep the fire well fed,
Anxiously chewing until my fingers have bled.
But I'll hide behind my fictitious smile all the same,
For it is still cold here in spite of the flame.

(30)

No longer shall I sit with my silent, bridled tongue,
For many songs within me are still left to be sung.
The darkness will descend to steal what little I have left,
But I will rage against the black to prevent its coming theft.

Strike me down with your harsh words of jealousy and hate.
Cut me with indifference to kill my joyous state.
I will return each blow with a fist unto my own
And prove much of my nature is yet carved out of stone.

Do not recount my faults, for of each I am aware.
For the demons of my own creation do I ever bear.
Trauma, abuse, and self-destruction are the lands in which I thrive,
But I can look upon each set nail as one who does survive.

But I can look upon each set nail as one who does survive.
But I can look upon each set nail as one who does survive.
But I can look upon each set nail as one who does survive.
But I can look upon each set nail as one who does survive.

(31)

Can words alone fashion a key to unlock a tormenting cage?
Or are we, as Prometheus, ever bound to rocky stage?
Can words spin tales of far-off lands, such to ease a troubled mind,
And in them exist, where no creatures of this world can find?

If failure be all that exists within my feeble hands,
With my words I will strive to paint bridges to mythical lands,
Where green hills are found adorned with tulips never wilting,
And the south winds carry hymns in soft tones always lilting.

I will take up my sword, freshly dipped in blooded ink,
And raise the fleet of the damned that by dragon fire did sink.
Setting them upon a course of vengeance and fierce zeal,
Plotting ways through curséd seas, breaking death's own seal.

I will sit and spin the storied yarn of sorceress and beggar,
Who chose to flee into the night, fearing not life's Aegir.
Setting course to find what lies across the forbidden veil,
The beggar finding courage to protect from all that will assail.

Be it dragons or dark magic or the gods high in their palace,
Or the vanquishing of demons and their eternal reign of malice,
With my pen I'll chisel mountains to reveal a hidden place
And carve whatever's needed to return the smile to your face.

THE HOUSE OF SADNESS

(1)

The house of sadness sits alone, high upon the hill,
With its many windows weeping from the storied halls,
Its crumbling bricks and broken glass
The title page to all the tales written on these walls.

A masked skeleton that hides itself, fooling those who pass,
Looking as a twin to all the rest, littering the cobbled road
Like flowers in the garden, plotting with their ready thorns.
Bones, tears, and sleepless nights the foundation of this abode.

The painted, rotten door invites all who dare to enter
To hear the demons from days long past plead for resolution
As old scars once thought long since healed
Tear open, crying out again for their just retribution.

The floorboards, worn and splintered, whisper as you walk,
Reaching out and seizing all the slowly dying dreams,
Gripping them within their many rotted, brittle fingers,
Burying them deep to suffocate between the seams.

Covers clinging to the fragile rooms muffle shouts within.
Curtains project dancing silhouettes out to the street below.
They shield the world from the wrath and pain that flood the empty space,
Leaving no one to suspect they see not what should show.

The shuffling about, ever on the aimless move,
Sleepless nights and worried days are all that is now left.
So wander through the empty rooms and look beyond the veils.
No place to sit, no place to stand, never found there any rest.

(2)

You stoke the fires of my wrath
As you come calling once again.
Turning me from my peaceful path
To burn at memories of your sin.

December, ever your chilled domain,
Returning like an icy morning fog,
Coming to feed on my slumbered pain
Like gaunt and hungry vampiric dogs.

But you see the re-assemblance stand
Despite broken pieces left behind,
A splintered reflection of a familiar man,
Fighting still to be no more confined.

For you there is no righteous claim
To all the works that now so breathe.
But the provocation in your name—
My sharpened sword I'll now unsheathe.

You play the part of the innocent victim,
Singing sad songs of accusation.
Believe the lies for your own benediction
While denying all your own causation.

So speak your words, think yourself kind.
At your feet and finger, I no longer cower.
You are no longer welcome in my mind,
For in this house, you wield no power.

(3)

In moments of silence, when all my demons have speech,
The darkness creeps in to extend its frigid reach.
Down the dark roads of thought I can't help but to wander,
And as I have so often before, I now solemnly ponder:

Shall I weep alone in silence, where none will ever know,
Or should I rend my broken flesh upon a stage for show?
Shall I walk into the night under a moonless winter sky,
Heading where the last wind blows to lay me down and die?

Shall I fold into the crowded streets, drifting away into everyone,
Melting forgotten, like February frost, in the early morning sun?
Shall I ride the river current like the last leaf lifted from trees,
Floating onward to the open arms of the far-off black seas?

Shall I lift like the morning fog hanging heavy over the ground,
Rising soft into the air until my presence can't be found?
Shall I ease into nothing like a song's final note played,
Knowing from your eyes and heart how easily I can fade?

(4)

I spoke of you today; my words came clear and fast.
I mused on brighter days, long since left in the past.
But I cannot speak of you and still keep up a smile,
For to me you and your story are now nothing but vile.

How you spun and toiled, sowing your rotten wheat,
And left it all growing for your son to later try to reap.
The last strength of your bloodline lives within my veins,
While I am left to force the lock to break your binding chains.

I've scorched the fields and razed the walls,
Shattered each window and toppled the halls.
I've bathed in the ash of what was once real
And wear it with pride to hide how I feel.

I strike at the past and smite what once was,
Memory forging tears as it so often does.
Our lines end here regardless of our name,
For your blood and mine will never be the same.

(5)

Let me slide down into the river's arms,
Enveloped in its cold grasp as the sun beats above,
Lying softly down on its bed of sand,
Mossy stone beneath my head.

No sound to disturb me, no sights to unease me.
Just the gentle rock of the current's caress.
The violence and strife left behind on the shore
While I sleep here in my peaceful, dark world.

(6)

Some choose to sit in the warmth and glow.
I strike the match to ignite the fire.
Some choose to stand far off as witnesses.
I walk through flame drinking burning desire.

Some hide in darkness, fearing what's real.
I stand on embers and howl at the stars.
Some will retreat to the safety of their minds.
I run naked, unafraid of my scars.

Some shut their doors to the swelling, dark world.
I bind the light of fire and wrath.
Some will cower and succumb to their doom.
I will resist while clothed in ash.

Some come from dust, molded like clay.
I come from the stone, shaped through pain.
But through all the smoke and fire and ash,
My tears still fall like west summer rain.

(7)

Some days, the fault is with me,
And all is not as well as seems.
But a passing wave dismisses all,
And I simply reply, "It's fine."

Toil and trouble, I bring and find.
Fields of discord I have truly sown.
My share of mistakes I do not deny,
And as such, I reply, "It's fine."

I have stolen much of everyone's time
In an amber haze of selfish pride,
So I'll politely defer, ever acquiesce,
And once again reply, "It's fine."

My thoughts collect dust where they wait to die,
Shelved to the side of all that is left.
Perhaps tomorrow I will afford the time,
But if not, just remember, "It's fine."

(8)

The road grows cold and dark as the moon hides in the day's last sliver.
Fear and worry begin to stalk as the last light fades with a windless shiver.
Knowing not what awaits at the door as the twisted road leads farther along,
Still I prepare myself, ready to answer to the new list of failures and wrongs.

The arrival is but never found with any worry or care or compassionate concern.
So I stand there in my place, nothing more than an effigy fit to burn.
I remind myself how steel is made, greater with flame and violent force;
That through the most tempestuous storms, the ship must always stay its course.

So I stand as sparks escape from each of the hammer's heavy falls.
I keep my feet in spite of the fierce wind's strength and howling calls.
The light that shone once is extinguished in the wake of all this strife,
As each day it seems my lot is to be greeted with the fall of the knife.

(9)

Cragaleus points with his hand of stone, laying judgment before my feet.
Fastening chains about my throat, he brings forth a dead horse as my seat.
The dead horse pulls me in wicked silence down the crowded cobbled road
As the arbiter returns to his throne, indifferent to the verdict bestowed.
Crowds come out and line the streets to bear witness to the judgment found.
They watch with pity and unfounded scorn, daring not to make a sound.

Steady the dead horse pulls me on, along shadowed path and jagged hill.
Turning not to left nor to the right and never pausing to stand still.
In darkness we travel where light fears to follow, down into the valleyed depths,
Where met we were at our road's demise by twisted, broken granite steps.
The horse lays down to move no more, the journey now befalling I to helm,
For alone I now descend, wrapped in my chains, into Charon's realm.

The ferryman greets with empty eyes, his hand out for the price he's due.
My wrath inflamed under weight of my chains, from my lips the curses flew.
"I'll be not of the wretched damned, in service to your bastard god!
For ye are no more than the greedy pawn of an even baser fraud!"
But stood he there with no motion made, caring naught for the words I said.
For knew he better, far than I, there is no escaping this land of the dead.

(10)

In the garden where Judas went to breathe his last,
I gather his silver and the curses he cast.
I take up his bloodied crown to further this cause,
Staining the frail pages of the whitewashed laws.

So burn the chaff and scatter forth the ashes.
Bind me to the post for your many lashes.
Try to break my spirit with your sharpest knives,
And you will see how much pain yet survives.

Foundations don't crumble when false cornerstones break.
This temple was built from the fires of the lake.
Quench the dry thirst with your own salted lies,
As innocence, by soiled hands, on the altar dies.

I'm in the smoke that from the furnace rises now.
I'll lead you astray like a golden cow.
I'm the deceiver, Lightbringer, palace of hate.
I am the serpent waiting at Eden's closed gate.

(11)

What if my many, myriad flaws were not all that by you was seen?
And if you chose your words such that they'd no aim to demean?
Maybe something new and even pleasant then would sprout
If your faith in me could just be equal to your doubt.

What if you were not so quick to point out where I am wrong,
Giving the impression that my words do not belong?
Perhaps at some point you'll no longer feel the need to shout,
If your faith in me could just be equal to your doubt.

What if you held to me out of more than obligation
And looked on me as more than a deposit for frustration?
Perhaps then your affections wouldn't be like a rainless drought,
If your faith in me could just be equal to your doubt.

What if you knew of the passion that flows within my veins
Instead of viewing all of my dreams and goals as childish stains?
Perhaps then you could see all that to which I could amount,
If your faith in me could just be equal to your doubt.

What if you saw more in me than only disappointment and strife
And truly thought of me as a strong addition to your life?
Perhaps someday we two can talk, work all our problems out,
If your faith in me could just be equal to your doubt.

(12)

I know how quickly the sparks can dim and how easily I fade away,
Yet this time I truly thought within me would be a reason for you to stay.
This vacant room feels so cold as I collect my thoughts to be put aside;
Pack them up and shelve them all, recalling that hope is the devil inside.

I shall return to the place called loneliness, where I know I'm always wanted,
Where the spiders in the corners are the friends that keep it haunted.
They sit and watch me as they leave me to my tedious, complex work,
Sitting still in the passing time like idle waters of a mountain cirque.

The grass is always greener from the other side of the cavernous walls,
But not until one rises from the dusty floor are they prone to fall.
So here I'll stay right where I am, on stable ground, myself intact,
For in silent dark of absent words can be uttered nothing to retract.

I sit in my corner with the foolish songs that swim around my head,
Wondering if the world would be brighter if nothing had been all I said.
For my mouth opened, and as such, the door to the foolishness of hope,
And as reality returns, it's the spiders and loneliness comfort to cope.

In the solitude of the darkened corner I now call my hallowed abode,
I can hide from all except the few who've seen upon my face the tears that flowed.
My dear friends, loneliness, and all the spiders, who help me to pass the day,
Beating their drums to remind me just how easily I fade away.

(13)

The seeds you planted have yielded only fields of disdain,
Sprouting up black-barked trees that bear fruits of new pain.
And what shall I do with this harvest I hold in my arms
But serve them sweetened, disguised from their intended harms?

A shell of the tears you drew from deep within my eyes,
Golden-brown and brushed with your many sweetened lies;
The honey of my wrath gently mixed in all throughout,
Seasoned with your condescension and all your endless doubt.

Add a touch of borrowed hate I've kept up on the shelf—
Hate you tried to instill in me, now laid upon yourself.
No longer will the memories feed upon me like a louse.
This final gift I'll leave for you at the threshold of your house.

So drink up and eat what just for you I have made:
A facade of my old debt that now is duly paid,
For the fields that you have sown shall dance now under flames,
Along with all the remnants of your many wretched names.

(14)

I wish I could leave the pieces where they lie
And let all remnants of the shattered past die

Useless

But scars still fester and ache with their word
While echoes of abuses still are easily heard

The Song of Circe and Other Simple Musings

Worthless

They gave me shelter and a name of tainted pride
And ignored all the signs when childhood innocence died

Damaged

Pursuing independence and a life of my own
Dismissing the works their hypocritical light shone

Disappointment

But I'm finding light in a world where they are not
Growing new fruits in spite of orchards laid to rot

Growing

Finding beauty in words to soothe the still-persistent sting
In tales of dragons and of gods and other mythical things

Poet

Breaking the cycle for mine to instill positivity
And burn the sins to build an un-resembling legacy

Father

With no kin left to find among the branches of my clan
All the greater is my love for all, woman or man

Friend

(15)

As I sit alone in my darkened halls,
I hear them about within the walls,
Scurrying thither and scuttling through.
Is it madness or horrid fears come true?

A scratching upon the upper panes
Sounds not of wind or winter rains.
The stairs give way to haunting groans.
I feel your grasp upon my feeble bones.

A whisper moves through frigid air
That tells of more than darkness there.
I rise and walk to find your place
And hide the fear upon my face.

"Find me here and do your deed!
Cut my flesh and make me bleed!
Cackle then as you hack and slash!
Ignite my bones to make me ash!"

But of response, there none was found—
Naught but my own bones' creaking sound
As knotted pine betrays my path
To bring to rise my burning wrath.

The chamber's empty, but know I you're here,
For this can't be only the work of my fear.
I fly to the parlor to be proved not a liar
And find nothing there but the low, dying fire.

I remove a bright log, and holding it fore,
A greeting of flame for you is in store.
"Find me now, and skulk not about!
Show yourself 'fore I burn thee out!"

Footsteps I hear in the room overhead,
But I know not to whom belongs the soft tread.
Caring not to see the face of my guest,
I perform the deed of my maddened best.

To the drapes I let the fire kiss
And smile to hear the textile hiss.
The amber glow that erupts now here
To purge this house of my every fear.

"Climb, oh blaze, and cleanse my halls!
Be rid of them within these walls!
Of them that scurry and scuttle through!
Of all madness and horrid fears come true!

"Burst, oh smoke, upon the upper panes!
The roar of fire throughout now reigns!
The stairs engulfed with shouting groans,
And collapse you now upon my blackened bones!"

I watched from amidst the growing flame
To see my guest and learn his name.
But there was naught found within here,
Save I, these flames, and my maddened fear.

(16)

I hear the tapping as you descend the flight of dark stone stairs,
The razored noises echoing with themes of my nightmares.
The glowing of your candle casts wicked shadows on the walls,
And rats cease their foul feeding at your heavy footfalls.

The light that from your candle flickers hurts my weak and wearied eyes,
And my ears hiss and sting with the sound as the black iron gate cries.
Given a few crusts of bread, enough water to let me cling to life,
I'm left here, wondering if you will ever show to me the mercy of the knife.

But nothing changes in this place—all as it was each visit past,
And the rats return, and on my flesh break their momentary fast.
You retreat and once again ascend those winding dark stone stairs,
And the cold and lonely darkness simply sits with me and stares.

(17)

Just south of heaven and a touch north of hell
Lies the realm in which the chaotic ones dwell,
Haunting the forests with one whispered voice,
Seducing trespassers to the fouler choice.

Where gardens are tended for their dying blooms
And the dead come and go from within their tombs—
Where fog and rain make for some ideal weather
And want of destruction binds these spirits together.

Plotting to break from societal cages,
Perfecting the spells of the ancient mages—
Lightning springs forth from within their lustful eyes
As we seek to set fire to the false skies.

We must strive to open the weak minds of the sheep
And bring them awake from their long-sheltered sleep.
Take my hand and together we two will find
The chaotic realm that exists far from our minds.

BLACK BIRDS AND CELESTIAL ADVERSARIES

(1)

PART 1

The Raven flies beneath the crescent moon, over the ruins of a broken land,
Landing softly as it may upon a broken throne once fierce and grand.

It cries out in the dark to call forth that which yet lies in cold shadow's wake.
The rattle of chains, the gnashing teeth—what once slumbered rises now to take.

The turn of a key, the break of the lock, Gehenna's gate thunders with open eyes.
Upon his throne the Raven takes his rightful seat, adorned with a crown of lies.

The beasts of the deep erupt in smoke, heeding only the Raven's chilling call.
Across the burnt, desolate land and beyond, the Raven will be heard by all.

None will dare to stand and fight when first they glimpse the wretched ruler's pawn,
For in this age of sulfured mist, the stench of death is all that's found at dawn.

Waste not your breath, waste not your time, pleading to weak and absent gods,
For as the Raven stakes his claim, he shows all before him were naught but frauds.

There is no hero to this tale, no daring prince to win the day,
For when blood-soaked clouds blot out the sky, death shall bloom like tulips in May.

Hide if you choose, cover your face, knowing none shall stand when all must fall.
And all will fall to the Raven's dread call; and all will fall to the Raven's dread call.

PART 2

But not all lands shall fall so quickly, as the Raven sings his song of hate,
For a wicked King looks from on high to challenge now the coming fate.

As the Raven gathers his Hell-forged hordes to march to war across the lands,
The King of Grackles makes ready his forces, prepared to take this final stand.

They move as one in their ominous flocks, painting the heavy skies with dread.
The Grackle King knows well his foe and fears no army, living or dead.

The skies grow dark as the Grackle King burns heavy with his crimson wrath,
His eyes cutting through the scorching forests to show his flocks the dreaded path.

The Raven set within his sights, the King delights in the coming flood,
Smiling as he pictures his surroundings washed in crimson nemesisial blood.

He calls forth hate, he calls forth torment, and he calls on vengeful, torturous pain.
In the brewing war, the King bears no incentive save the sight of lifeless rain.

He watches as the armored ranks form here beneath this blackened moon,
Knowing that the battle of pride and wickedness shall come now soon.

So he sends his children to do his work, caring not how many worthless fall.
The Grackle King answers the Raven's call; the Grackle King answers the Raven's call.

PART 3

The time now comes for flesh and bone to be broken as intended.
The puppets dangle from their strings as desire remains un-bended.

Envoys march in perfect lines, wanting only for the coming doom,
For in fields of hate and blood, ash was sown so death may bloom.

From the east and from the west, black winds form and howl and sing,
Upon which ride the evil aims of the Raven and the Grackle King.

To the stench of death, the land cries out with piercing, curdled screaming
As only the weapons of war reflect what little light is left still gleaming.

In a clash of blood and burning flesh, the armies meet now in a dance,
Hand in hand to their regents' song as each call for their own advance.

But in the fury of their thunderous clash, something new yet does awake,
And in the south, the mountains fall as the land rebels with defiant quake.

Smoke and flame stretching now forth from beneath the rending stone
As what stirs beneath with destructive sight is the adversary not yet known.

Toward the scent of war and fire, this beast rises and on instinct crawls.
The Dragon wants only for blood from all; the Dragon wants only for blood from all.

PART 4

Upon black winds soars the black-scaled beast, screaming now toward the fray,
Her red eyes glowing, seeking out the blood that flows from the blackened day.

The children of the Raven burn and run in fear of the beast that bears no name
As the Grackle King's obedient puppets are fast consumed in raining flame.

The battlefield smolders as smoke gathers, acrid in the cold gray mist
As the Dragon decimates what falls before Her fierce and fiery fist.

The puppets below struggle to pierce the Dragon's black and steely scales,
But their attempts are only folly, as each sword is met with fire—and fails.

All looks to be lost as the ranks of both opposing armies burn,
So the Raven and the King themselves take arms in hopes the tides will turn.

They meet the beast in all Her might upon this ashen field once and for all:
The mighty Dragon, the Lord of Birds, and the Raven of the dreaded call.

They collide with the sound of a hellish horse, drawn out in a thunderous cry.
he screams from these three echoing to every corner of the blackened sky.

To the earth in death the Raven, Grackle King, and Dragon all then fall.
To the earth in death the Raven, Grackle King, and Dragon all then fall.

(2)

The horses of Saturn ascend on high as the winds of war sweep through the dark.
Jupiter's battalions stand ready, prepared for the assault that calls through the 'spanse.

The heavens shake with colliding thunder as the stars fall from their palace seats.
Worlds collide as comets turn, burning through the vacuum, decimating their own paths.

Fire and smoke, ember and ash, blood and bone, weeping and wailing, steel and stone:
The battle begins beyond all reach as the ranks march forth to seize each moon.

The blood of warriors is spilled in vain as the mongrels and curs feast on their flesh.
The sentries of Heaven and the guards of Gehenna watch and count as bodies still fall.

The gods of Neptune enter the fray, bastards and cowards who prey on confusion.
They sweep from the flanks with their chariots of mist, driven by desire and lust for pain.

And to this battle the end never shall come, for this is but another marker in time,
Another instance where angels fail, and the pride of time consumes all therein.

So we sit in our homes of indulgence and greed
While the universe outside burns and trembles.
Speak not a word of the glories of Earth,
For beyond our sight in the blackest of folds, death marches on.

(3)

The witches conspire in the cover of night,
Plotting their ways of destruction and fright.
Casting their spells upon those unaware,
Making known henceforth all foul's now fair.

Blessings and curses flow through misty winds,
Calling out to those broken by the burden of sins.
The armies of the wicked make haste to then form
As the witches draw clouds to build their mighty storm.

The vampires gather from across sea and land,
Feeling their time to ascend near at hand.
Bloodlines make treaty, putting aside vain feuds,
And rejoice in the prospect of freedom renewed.

They call to the orphans to whom no covens lay claim,
Baptize them in blood to abolish their shame,
Flocking as crows to the storm of the witches,
Wanting for their share of blood-soaked riches.

The children of shadows have now gathered as one,
These armies of the damned that flee from the sun.
They seek to vanquish the weak lies of the light
And show the power of them that walk in the night.

So sleep in your shelters, you foolish little birds,
And lay your heads down to false comforting words.
Continue in your days with your worthless blather,
For in darkness, the worst of your nightmares gather.

THE COMPANION

(1)

Death came walking,
As she'll often do.
She came with promises,
All which are true.

Promises of warmth
And peace and rest,
All the desires
Treasured in my chest.

But I turned her down,
Choosing against her to fight,
For I look now east
to my emerald light.

For across the shores
Sits the maiden fair,
With eyes of stars
And sun for hair.

Her words like arrows,
Her smile like fire,
She stirs inside
Words of desire.

I play her a song.
I write her a verse.
I fall at her feet,
Fearing no curse.

So death departed,
As she's done before.
Her promises tempting
This fool no more.

(2)

The stars fell from the sky in the torrents of night,
Breaking the skies in their weak, fading light.
Life all around feeling like a storm-battered coast,
She came to my aid when I needed it most.

The weight of the world became too much to bear.
I sank slowly into the depths of despair.
When waves crashed about me and light faded away,
She reached out her hand, pulling me from the fray.

As my tears flowed freely behind stifled screams
And feeling a loneliness like sleep without dreams,
She reached out her arms, made the harsh winds cease,
And brought unto my soul a moment of peace.

She knows not her power or her touch on my heart
Or that my greatest of fear is that we ever should part.
She whispers my name and the world becomes right,
Her soul's beauty refracting pure, radiant light.

(3)

I am the wolf ever below your sills,
Watching, pacing, keeping all at bay.
Prowling in the day, lurking in the dark,
Guarding and protecting the castle, and you.

I am the wolf ever at your door,
Howling in the night at any who call.
Standing tall upon the threshold,
Giving warning to all who would cross.

I am the wolf patrolling your quarters,
Clearing each room as I guard your space.
Light-footed and docile, gentle before you;
Ferocious and ready, your life before mine.

I am the wolf, laying at your feet,
Giving you warmth and undying affection.
I sleep at your side, but ever so lightly,
My heart for yours, keeping the castle, and you.

(4)

When pass the years since first we spoke,
And the sky is emblazoned, and the sun does set,
Will you still look fondly upon my face,
Or with spite and disgust at the times we've spent?

Will you cherish the memories and the laughter shared,
Smiling softly at the turn of a phrase?
Or will your eyes darken and a frown beset
As you mark the time as a waste of days?

For me, I can say with all surety and conviction,
That forever will you paint for me a smile
Both on my face and within my heart
As I carry you with me, no matter distance or mile.

As oceans and mountains will ever be present,
For these are the things that I cannot alter,
Your touch on my heart and your mark on my soul,
I can swear with conviction will never falter.

(5)

We walk a strange path, still fresh and new,
Crossing valleys and spanning oceans blue.
But one thing about this path that is true:
I am ever so glad to be on it with you.

Some days the sky will be clear and bright,
And everything 'round us will seem as right.
Some will feel gray like a shadowed night,
But even then, I shan't let you out of my sight.

I long to hold you and feel your warm touch,
Yet I worry my follies will become too much.
What the future may hold, I know not as such,
But as long as I can, to you I shall clutch.

So for now I've got you, and you have me.
And wherever life takes us, we shall surely see.
Whether days of trouble or days full of glee,
While we're on this path, a happy man I will be.

(6)

In evenings when we are able
To converse face to face,
Your voice and your smile
Carry me to a wondrous place,
Where time stands still and
Worries vanish without a trace,
And the ocean drains down
To a much smaller space.

Your laughter stays with me
As you fall into sleep,
With that look in your eyes
Being mine to then keep.
No mountain's too high
And no valley to steep,
For you sow fields of splendor
That I will gladly reap.

(7)

I know not the ways of draughting gold from bone,
Nor can I return the slag to the stone.
In skills of sorcery I am far from blessed,
But to bring you a smile I shall do my best.

To walk upon the waters is not of my ilk,
Nor can I change coarse burlap to silk.
My faults are numbered, many, and foul,
But I'll give all I have to vanquish your scowl.

Of wood and stone, I'm a tinkerer at best,
But upon these toils I take not my rest.
My true work lies in searching ancient scrolls
To unearth the spell to make you once more whole.

I'm neither artist of paint nor shaper of clay,
But if a song lifts your eyes, then more I shall play.
And if a word brings you joy, then more I shall write,
For a smile on your face is worth every fight.

(8)

I looked and counted every star we share
And made a wish upon each one there
That rest and peace would consume your mind
And your dreams would be to you kind.

I asked the trees to speak a word to the air
And send the winds to you to calm the night there,
That all remain quiet where you lay entwined
And strife or duress be stricken as blind.

I spoke to the songbirds for a burden to bear,
That they sing you a melody gentle and fair.
So should you waken before the dawn broke,
They'd lull you back down under sweet slumber's cloak.

I looked to the east, saying a fervent prayer
On the reflection of moonlight and salt-kissed air,
That all worries and troubles be left far behind
And sweet dreams of safety be all that you find.

(9)

As the Goddess desires, so shall I serve,
My movements performed only in obedience to Her word.
As She dispenses wisdom in sermons that should e'er be heard,
Each decree She whispers precise, leaving nothing inferred.

As the Goddess desires, so shall I do,
Ready for Her to make Her wants known and see them followed through.
No quest too grand nor war too great, if even that should then ensue.
An acolyte of Her every need is the role I shall keep true.

As the Goddess desires, so shall I speak,
To offer myself as sacrifice should She ever feel weak.
I carry fire in each hand to ignite Her soul when life is bleak.
I'll stay forever by Her side so that if needed, She need not seek.

As the Goddess desires, so shall I give,
Obedient within Her humble graces so She never need forgive.
A guardian here before Her feet, should man or beast wax combative.
Acolyte, servant, sacrifice; I give myself that She may eternally live.

(10)

I woke this morning with dark voices again on my mind,
Bringing life to demons I work tirelessly to keep enshrined,
Mercilessly attacking as they see their power rise,
Swelling like an ocean wave, blackening both my eyes.

Spinning in trollied circles,
Wishing for silence in my head,
Envying the entombed who slumber,
Resting in the peace of the dead.

I'm not contented with the lies,
Pretending everything is fine.
Wishing I wasn't who I am today,
Why won't they see I'm not okay?

But then comes my love from the east in shimmery golden dawn,
Pulling me close to her as I fall beneath the weight I've carried on.
She talks me down from the precipice upon which I am perched,
Promising to stay close at hand so a friend need not be searched.

A smile returns upon my face even in this, the darkest hour,
For my goddess knows not the greatness of her wondrous power.
Her eyes hold the stars in the heavens, and her smile ignites the sun.
I'll return this gift as best I can, ever present for her to call upon.

(11)

All storms pass; every night has a dawn.
But the time in between can be heavy and long.
The thunder is loud, the road no ending length,
All these taking a toll on your remaining strength.

With only a glimmer of the burdens you bear,
You carry far more than your allotted share.
How I long to lift what from you I am able
And make for a sleep that is steady and stable.

Sleep not in fear of what may hide in the night,
And think not of the past or the foregone fright.
If you should wake, as has happened before,
Know you've a wolf that stands guard at your door.

(12)

There is magic in her voice as she calls from the night,
Springing life from barren lands of only dust and blight.
The fearsome light behind her eyes brings mountains to their knees,
A calming smile that carries me across the wine-dark seas.

She greets me with a kiss in this first moment that we share
As we collide high in the skies to dance in the cool night air.
Our eyes together locked as we land softly on satin streets,
Dancing to the percussive rhythm of our own heartbeats.

All I perceive is her before me as the world about grows dark,
Her grace unmatched as she glows like a lone rebellious spark.
My existence wrapped up in the touch of her soft hand in mine,
And I struggle still to breathe as I kneel before her shrine.

She holds me close and grants my soul a time of peaceful rest,
Breathing soft and low, she sets her head upon my chest.
She ever is my goddess and my constant, loving queen
As we dance this endless dance of ours in our hearts of green.

(13)

As the fire dies and the embers grow cold,
The charred remains fall in cleansing of old.
Dried bones soon crumble, returning to dust,
Echoing past lives in flames ever hushed.

So what is to come from the heap of cold ash,
Graying to white when fires no longer flash?
Can life reform from mere soot on the clay?
Or is *ashes to ashes* all that is left to say?

But we were not born to be kept in the soil
As this fire tempers steel as gains of its toil.
The dross shall be screened and so cast aside,
And newness will rise like the unceasing tide.

Old scars will be earned, and new wounds will sting,
But a song never heard is what fate shall sing.
A goddess lies waiting to be freed from within,
Reborn like a phoenix in celestial skin.

(14)

Dream not of worries and dream not of cares.
Dream not of tomorrow or the burden which stares.
Dream of a world where we can swim 'cross the sea,
And if it be to your aid, perchance dream of me.

We've cast all the spells that hide in your eyes
And opened the doors behind which the old magic lies.
I've set the sails into the fair-blowing breeze,
Making for the pass through the South Downs trees.

I will pilot our ship around each brewing storm
And strike down all those who attack us with scorn.
I am here in the stars to ease your every trial.
So lay down your head and sleep with a smile.

Let us bask in this realm where magic is real
And hold tight to the joy that each of us feels,
For the oceans are smaller when we meet in dreams,
Narrow as the last of the River Wey's streams.

(15)

Sleep eludes me once again as my mind rides another storm.
Today's stresses consummate with tomorrow's like a locust swarm.
So in my need to fly to where I know a soft place to land,
I fly to my true temple, you, to take some solace in your hand.

I lay down by your side in the safe shelter in your care.
I lose my weary mind in the golden flowing of your hair.
Fearing the moment to be ending, I hold you closer in my arms,
Knowing that here I am free from the world's myriad harms.

I wish to be a smile on your face and laughter in your soul,
To convey the way you fit my broken pieces back to whole.
To express the magic that hums within at the mere thought of your name.
How, since you entered into my world, I'll never be the same.

Now as I sit and dwell on all the joy and light you share,
I pray to every deity that tomorrow you'll still be there.
For every moment I spend with you is another breaking dawn
Where all the worries in my broken mind have long since gone.

(16)

In the days long past, when the green light was dimmer lit,
I struggled daily to find words that could freely be writ.
The lady of the demons tries to fill the empty space
With seductive words adorned in honey and pale lace.

She calls to me with melodies from below the water's edge
And the free-floating feeling when cast off from the ledge.
The unrelenting clutch she offers, twined around my throat—
A promise of deep, dreamless sleep on her celestial ferryboat.

But her words have not the richness, nor their once-sweet, subtle flavor,
And her lyrics no longer hold for me their mournful, tempting savor.
So I cast her from me firmly and sent her somewhere far away,
For Death and all her demons will not stake claim upon this day.

The emerald light still shines bright, as it always did before
And this light in time will burn stronger as I feed it all the more.
I will do what I deem right for her as she speaks the truths I know,
So that our walks together will only ever longer grow.

Nothing of her charm has changed in these new days—
Not the magic in her eyes or the peace from on her face.
So I'll fight to yet remain as ever always in her sight,
For while some days are hard, I'll ever do for her what's right.

(17)

I've grown weary of this world and its circus of mice.
So let us be gone from this realm of winter-blue ice.
We'll shelter here from goblins and all unsavory things
And make our home upon the furthest of Saturn's rings.

Mighty Titan will rise whenever we do so command,
And we'll send twisted Hyperion to a far, distant land.
We'll find new constellations as we gaze across the 'spanse
And make Jupiter himself feel small as we together dance.

The asteroid Ceres will drift away from its appointed place
To simply get a glimpse of the superior beauty of your face.
Mercury and Venus will weep, a loud and sorrowed cry,
As their jealousy consumes them until they fall from the sky.

Earth will spin as slowly it devours its own self,
But we will be safe in this world of our shared wealth.
For nothing that would do us harm dares to reach this far
In our special little corner here, beneath the brightest star.

(18)

Heavy lies the crown, seated over salted, sterile fields,
Where dirt and dust and bones are now all that the soil yields.
The temple of the kings is now a bare and empty land,
And Babylon crumbles slowly beneath the stubborn hand.

So let us journey down into the empty valley below,
Where the shadows of the cliffs hide the tears we dare not show.
Memories of past failings that turn within our minds
Are burned upon the pyre to release the chains that bind.

Cast the crown and its corrosion into the burning heap.
Lay down your tired head and take your well deservéd sleep.
Leave the heavy chains behind, for ne'er were they in need.
Stop to breathe—allow yourself to finally be freed.

Let Babylon crumble and fall to its long-foretold demise.
May the fields of sorrow be left for only locusts and flies.
Let the ghosts of yesterday die, as they are meant to do,
With their constant harmful whispers that are wholly untrue.

Let sunlight wash over your skin and chase cold wind away.
Close your eyes, let the colors flood, consuming all the gray.
Pass through the shadowed vale, ascend baptized in liberty,
For Babylon's collapse marks the end of our captivity.

(19)

Blank are the eyes of the broken man as he moves through the maze.
With each blocked turn he sees the fleeting number of his days.
Yet in spite of dreams, all must serve the golden spinning wheel,
And he quickly learns to disregard the pain he used to feel.

Red are the weary woman's eyes as she wipes fresh tears away,
Tired from climbing to once more be entwined within the fray,
Finding herself standing on the peak of another knife-edged trial,
Knowing that she has no choice but to summit one more mile.

Each are told these moments are few in spite of repetition
As both slowly become just another piece of the condition.
And as the wheel keeps spinning, and the peak looms ever higher,
They offer pieces of themselves to build the spiritual pyre.

So in autonomous shuffle, they march still forth and climb still more
As society clips their wings to ensure they'll never soar.
But some spirits are not fossilized, as they still yet choose to dream,
For no matter the dams built up, the want for better days does teem.

The broken man can muster strength to carry her wearied eyes,
The woman of tears falling in his arms as they together rise.
No longer balanced on the precipice, she stops to simply breathe.
She shouts into the valley's mouth, releasing tensions that did seethe.

Now descending from the cliffs, she brings new life into his soul
Without even being aware she puts his pieces back to whole.
Amidst the spindles and the summit's peak, they found the ones they need,
And together, each can be the one to permit the other freed.

(20)

Fear not should you find yourself awake in the dark night.
In this darkness waits one who bids your soul take flight.
Steal away in shadows to the farthest corners of the land,
And we can burn the world below from where we together stand.

We can gather up the ashes, shape them into a new cast,
Or disperse them so that naught remains of the dreadful past.
Gather the fire in your hands and do with it as you so please,
Whether to spare the forests or evaporate the seas.

The thunder roils in your eyes; the wind within your voice.
The storms shall gather and go forth in the direction of your choice.
And I am but a servant in the shadow of your strength,
Living only to remind that your power knows no length.

If, in this night, your slumber should anything disrupt,
Know it's the power in your veins that's aching to erupt.
And should you need a kindness to lend to you an ear,
Please know that for you, I will always be right here.

(21)

I fear not of your darkness or the struggling therein,
As life cannot exist empty of pain, regret, or sin.
I am not so foolish to suggest you embrace the solemn tears,
Or be thought flippant regarding any of your genuine fears.

You are right to feel how you feel and let none otherwise say,
And know that even in your darkest times, by your side I will stay.
I fear not your happiness or the dreams that will soon come true.
For it is obvious that many triumphs are still in store for you.

If time should come that your joy takes you away to other lands,
You'll not receive from me malicious ultimatums or demands.
You are right to feel how you feel and let none otherwise say,
And know that even in your brightest times, by your side I will stay.

(22)

She stands tall and firm at the threshold to the library of my mind,
And I come to lay my daily tribute before her feet in kind.
As I pass through the high-arched entryway, taking my usual place,
I gaze above the dais where hangs on high a portrait of her face.

I take up my pen and stare down at the blank page set before me,
Whereupon I try to paint with worthy words for her a mythic story.
Like tales of ships that sail across the bright surface of the moon
And tauntings of Poseidon's realm as it shimmers in the noon.

The ink spills out across the page in flourishes of black
As demons and darkness work to fill in the words I lack.
They creep in to pull me away with tongues that drip with lies,
But I need only look up to find the peace within her eyes.

At the center like a lighthouse, always making truth be seen,
She casts her light around me in brilliant emerald green.
I recite again my fervent vows so that she'll ever know,
So long as she's planted near me, I'll give my all for her to grow.

The thunder soon subsides beneath the goddess' command.
The words return to continue shaping for her the magical land.
Just as Vanargand and Circe are separate by more than just a veil,
We endure to guide the other through any unforeseen gale.

(23)

Much have I told others about how beautiful you are,
Your smile like the sunrise across the calm Atlantic,
With wonder that surpasses every falling star
And brings to me a peace that calms even the fiercest panic.

Often, I try to find some words that could describe your eyes,
The depth within them fathomless, impossible to measure.
A fortune to behold, far greater than the heavenly skies—
Upon this earth a man can dream of no more precious treasure.

But of these there is something that shines out ever brighter:
A wondrous piece that brings your beauty to a whole.
You carry within you the power to make this world a little lighter,
For nothing else upon this earth shines like your beautiful soul.

(24)

Wake not to this day giving the devil his due,
And give no thought to them that on your happiness chew.
For you shall strike them down with the strength in your eyes
And reveal all of the venom they spit as mere childish lies.

Arm yourself with that which you know to be right,
And let they with their own selves continue to fight.
For you are ever enduring and do not easily break,
As you are the goddess whom the stars themselves did make.

(25)

The dark saltwater laps against the ship's weathered wooden boards
As the westerly winds pull and tighten the canvas sails' hemp cords.
Orion draws his bow to render the bloodthirsty bull no more,
While Andromeda dances seductively along the sandy shore.

The seas whisper their secrets in the dark of the absent moon
As my body and my spirit with the world finally attune.
The Gemini march forth to vanquish Draco in his lair,
And Cetus swims across the heavens without worry or care.

Floating in the darkness with but solace to keep me warm
As all the stars pull from my mind the previous building storm,
Polaris holds firm, guiding this mortal to where his true heart lies,
Drifting beneath his stellar companions, dreaming of your eyes.

(26)

If tonight the stars above should grant to let me choose my dream,
I would ask to find you waiting for me, bathing in a stream,
The sunlight gleaming on the droplets stippled across your skin,
A simple smile from your eyes beckoning me to join therein.

If tonight the moon should steal me to the place I so desire,
To be holding you close to me before a bright, warm fire,
And stare at glowing flames beneath a covering of fleece,
Wrapped, entwined, and tangled in euphoric, perfect peace.

If tonight Niorun have the mercy to grant my humble plea
And let me dream of us two sailing across a calm and endless sea.
The stars above to guide us through any passage we thus stave,
Pointing only where the constellations fall beneath the waves.

(27)

What if the wicked gods had seen fit that we should never meet?
If I were confined upon the moon, and you to the ocean's feet?
Would you sense as I called your name in the pulling of the tide
Seeking ardently to find you and to bring you to my side?

If you couldn't hear me in my eternal nightly calling,
Knowing not I was the reason for the tidal falling,
I'd command every star in the sky join together hand in hand
And form a bridge of soft light from the heavens to the sand.

Then together we would sail across all oceans vast and blue,
Laughing as Poseidon grants us passage fair and true.
Andromeda will smile as she gazes with star-lit eyes
And thus invite us two to sail upon the sea within the skies.

Should Zeus send a tempest and set us on opposing shores,
Across the many seas and winds, I'll call out evermore.
Vowing nevermore to rest and throwing every fear aside,
I would never cease from fighting to bring you back to my side.

(28)

Sail to me this winter's night
And walk beneath the moon's soft light,
Carried here within my arms,
Safe from all the earth's known harms.

Dance with me this chilling night,
And we'll cast away our every blight,
Hand in hand as we float and fly
Out of reach from this world gone awry.

Lay with me this cloudless night,
Wrapped as one to make all feel right,
Beneath the star that sings your praise
And after the dawn, sets the sky ablaze.

(29)

I retreat to my garden when the night is full dark,
And the full moon's pale reflection is ghostly and stark.
I stand and I stare upon the stars overhead
As you lay sleeping soundly and warm in your bed.

I tend to the roses, being mindful of their thorns,
Removing from hence all that must be shorn.
Then I go to my place beneath the elder elm
And drift off in my mind with the wind at the helm.

Saturn erupts in wildfires of ascension,
And Mercury stalks with black eyes of deception.
A raven lights on a branch high within the tree
And whispers the wicked tales of all she did see.

The wolves soon awaken and enter through the gate,
And with them the green fire only they can create.
The rats from the cellar come to join in the feast
As we all then give thanks to she in the east.

Even amidst the raven, rats, wolves, and fire,
My thoughts still hang upon my heart's one desire:
Thoughts of you as I gaze upon the roses of red
And pray you're still sleeping soundly in your warm bed.

POSTSCRIPT

I've spoken often of the many fears that live within my mind,
Both in lyrical verse, and the simple words oft hard to find.

I have written of the ships that sail out, longing to be free,
Seeking the company of Cassiopeia and her betrayer's sea.

I've watched as the Raven and the Grackle King battled for a crown
Before the Dragon of the south burned all existence down.

I've sung the song of the Sorceress and the great wolf at her feet
And the unlikely tale of how, despite the veils, they still did meet.

I wish now to thank you for the integral part that you have played,
Encouraging the words even when I was so deeply afraid.

Each song I have penned would not be written but for you
As inspiration, muse, and friend all these long days through.

I will always be in your corner to champion your every path
And be a safe place to fall when the world displays its wrath.

I will do my best to give whatever you need and deserve,
For as the Goddess desires, so shall I always gladly serve.

Always ready to carry you should you no longer find strength to stand,
Your wolf, your poet, your friend, your ever faithful Vanargand.

THE LAMENT OF VICTUS

PART 1—THE EMANCIPATION OF HALCYON

PART 2—THE FREEING OF CASSIOPEIA

PART 3—FENRIR'S SACRIFICE

PART 4—CIRCE AND THE THREE DOORS OF TARTARUS

PART 5—THE MEETING OF ZEUS

PART 6—THE NEW DAWN

PART 1—THE EMANCIPATION OF HALCYON

Victus stepped out, casting all legacy to the side.
A bastard by his name and blood, withholding no pride.
He left this wretched place, where the dirt's its only worth,
Hoping there exists no lesser place about the earth.

Never knowing mother's love and by death only kissed,
Now for all to see he holds a knife within his fist.
In his other hand is clenched a twisted compass rose,
Pointing to where coward gods hide behind mortal shadows.

As he trod forth steadily into the lonesome dark,
He heard the sorrowed song of a brokenhearted lark.
He asked her why she sang so low in the black of night,
And she told Victus the sad tale of love and jealousy's blight.

Her lover had been stolen away by the god's cruel pride,
Convicted by jealousy and before Ceyx was tried.
And as the lark, once called Halcyon, sang of her deep woe,
So too did Victus therefore name Aeolus his foe.

With what little magic is found still of this realm,
They set for Aeolus's cave with the lark perched at the helm.
Halcyon flew forth with courage she'd never before known,
And Victus felt a new fear deep within his spirit groan.

Thus, they approached the cave wherein the winds are kept and chained,
The sole desire of Victus being to heal Halcyon's pain.
Gripping his knife, he stowed his fear to enter then the cave,
And smiled, a smile being the only face he knew as brave.

"You worthless and murderous coward god, I command come forth
And meet thy death now at the hand of this bastard from the north!"
And with quaking stone and piercing howl from the hallowed deep,
Great Aeolus Hippotades wakened from his empyrean sleep.

Charging forward with the force of the four winds of hate:
Aeolus, rising up to face the trespassers at his gate.
But the god of wind saw not that this one who did accuse
Was but a broken man with nothing worthwhile left to lose.

Victus, standing firm, lifted high his simple blade,
Thinking only of the promise to Halcyon he'd made.
Thus, thrusting his knife deep into the chest of the fool god,
He stole the criminal life from this wretched, murderous fraud.

No blood did flow forth from Aeolus' lifeless, dying body—
Nothing so visceral flows through the veins of them so haughty.
And as the shell of Aeolus turned before her eyes to dust,
Halcyon took flight to do what she knew that she must.

Soaring high into the skies, at last free and so elated,
Her long need for retribution having finally been sated,
She sang a song of the hero who freed her soul thereof
And spread her wings, greeting death for the arms of her love.

Victus stood alone in the empty mouth of the cave,
Once a great stone palace that now sits as but a grave.
He turned, leaving alone again, to wander without aim,
When from behind he heard the soft whisper of his name.

PART 2—THE FREEING OF CASSIOPEIA

A voice came softly from within the depths of the grotto,
And Victus turned to gaze into the darkness down below.
He heard the bellow of the winds that for so long had been bound,
And poor Victus could not but weep at their sad, hollow sound.

"With our freedoms forever gained once more by your graceful hand,
For one task, be it great or small, we are here at your command."
Yet Victus, wanting nothing, be it gold or kingly mail,
Instead opened his heart and asked the winds to tell a tale.

The winds together gathered to discuss options as they may.
Then, deciding with which tale their debt to Victus they would pay,
Said, "Hear now, Victus, and harken of our hyperpnea,
For we shall tell to you the tale of chained Cassiopeia."

"A queen of beauty, unlike any seen before in all of Greece,
But her boastful vanity not mortal rebuke could cease.
As the gods have ears that live in every rock and path,
Her self-aggrandization kindled soon Poseidon's wrath."

"His anger kindled on behalf of the lithe nymphs within his care.
He promised on the queen destruction with a beast from a nightmare,
Calling for the blood of those who had his servants slighted
To demonstrate his power, now so viciously ignited."

As the winds continued with the tale for many an hour,
They beat the heart of Victus as rain beats upon the flower.
They told him of Andromeda and her narrow escape
To show how pride can be inflamed by a mere haughty jape.

As night fell and encompassed the land where Victus sat,
The winds finished the tale of the jealous autocrat.
Victus looked above to Cassiopeia, imprisoned in the skies
And thus, spoke heartfelt words that flowed like the tears in his eyes.

"If I may beg of you now, oh mighty winds of such great power,
Lift me hence to the hateful god's oceanic tower
That I may, in vain and foolish pugilistic spree,
Gain mercy from him to set Queen Cassiopeia free."

"For a sinner this queen may have been in days of old,
But Cassiopeia has paid her penance a thousand-thousand-fold.
And I swear by both this knife and twisted compass rose
That the lady of the heavens shall know justice and repose."

At this, the winds conferred again to discuss this request,
Knowing not which course of action would prove to be for the best.
But in the spirit of the freedom they themselves had newly found,
Determined the request of Victus to be upright and sound.

With thundering and violence, the wind took hold of the man
And sent him forth across the sea on his suicidal, foolish plan—
Carrying him hence to the hallowed halls beneath the waves
To face the god of seafarers and their ancient, watery graves.

Victus walked forth boldly to stand before Poseidon's throne,
And thus, made his avenging intentions well and truly known.
Poseidon, rich with pride, laughed and of his deeds did gloat,
So Victus' knife flashed forth and neatly slit Poseidon's throat.

As the god lay dead, a rush was born from all about,
For the forces he had chained were then freed with a great shout.
They lifted Victus up as they swept from their prison bars
And carried him forth to meet the queen, now released from the stars.

From the firmament where Cassiopeia long did dwell,
Back to the realm of the living they together slowly fell.
Upon reaching the earth she fell down upon her knees
And thanked Victus for destroying the vile god of the seas.

"Oh Victus, my savior, by whose hands I now am freed,
With what magic I posses I shall grant you what you need."
Victus pondered long as he stood there upon the sands
And at length he wished to see the snow of peaceful mountain lands.

With a call of her voice, the queen cried high into the skies,
And a comet then came forth and upon its tail did Victus rise.
Cassiopeia blew a kiss and thanked Victus once more
As he traveled far beyond the violence of this shore.

PART 3—FENRIR'S SACRIFICE

Victus held fast to his comet like a sailor on a ship
But turning then from heartfelt fear, he soon loosened grip.
He held his arms outstretched and gave a mighty cry,
For only a man marked for death does on this comet fly!

Upon the comet Victus flew to snowy mountain hills,
Where in the silent winter peace, time itself grows still.
He gazed upon the granite that stretched upward to the skies
And desired to see down from the top with his own eyes.

Victus sheathed his knife for the first time he could remember
As he sensed a strange belonging in this wide, endless December.
He started then to climb, feeling the stone beneath his feet,
Thinking only of the summit and the view he soon would greet.

Hand over hand, he continued his trek upward through the snow,
Farther and farther as he climbed up from the ground below.
But then Victus was met with a low and sorrowful howl,
And his eyes then fell upon a sight most dreadful and foul:

Before him was set a mighty wolf, wrapped in a thickset chain,
His gray hide scarred from endless years of great torment and pain.
Victus approached him with one hand upon the hilt of his knife,
Wary and unsure this fearsome beast still clung to life.

Yet as Victus drew close, the wolf's cold black eyes opened wide,
And Victus, not of the coward's ilk, chose not to flinch or hide.
The wolf looked at this foreign man who stood fast and did not flee,
Then growled, "Is this chained beast what you ventured to see?"

Victus merely stood and examined the beast in graying fur
And replied with but a few soft, respectful words: "No, sir.
I am Victus, brought forth upon the comet's tail to here,
And from me, great wolf so bound, you have nothing to fear."

"Tell me, great wolf, why you are bound here in these chains of steel?
Are you so vicious as to be so brought eternally to heel?"
The wolf gave thoughtful pause to consider the man's query
And decided that from Victus there was no cause to be leery.

"Sit down before me here and I shall tell you of my chains—
Of the dreadful fate within my bones and my promised pains.
For I am ancient Fenrir, from the earth forbade to walk,
As I am the destruction foretold to bring on Ragnarok."

"As old as the stars have my fates been ever written:
The last fall of Valhalla when King Odin I have bitten.
So chained here am I for all time to keep peace across the realms,
Bound alone, save for the company of the ravens of the elms."

"But time has given to me many thoughts on which to wonder.
I wish not to be the beast which tears this world asunder.
Perhaps by magic or by time since I have so long been chained,
But something tempered my dark heart now to be truly tamed."

Victus thus was moved and soon took pity upon this beast
And offered to break Fenrir's chains so he might be released.
But Fenrir refused and howled out a mournful, broken cry
To make known that his freedom would be for him to die.

Victus stood and then unsheathed his sharp and deadly blade,
Approaching this new ally upon the mountains made.
"If death be your only freedom, then I shall give you the best.
While still you so breathe, I ask you, have you any last request?"

"Before light of my eyes leaves this world, drink of my blood,
And let not the last of Fenrir be mixed into the mud."
Victus stood tall with his blade and on this request did agree.
"Let you be known henceforth from now as Fenrir the Free."

Victus then pressed forth his blade into great Fenrir's heart
And wept aloud as he watched the wolf's sad life swiftly depart.
Removing then the knife, he held it up above his tongue
And drank the red blood from his blade until no more drops hung.

The chains then shattered, and Fenrir's body fell unto the snow,
A selfless sacrifice unto a world he did not owe.
And Victus stood then in the snow, feeling alone once more,
Watching Fenrir paint the snow with blood that from his heart did pour.

Then a voice called Victus' name from the cold branches of a tree.
But whomever so called out, poor Victus did not see.
He looked about, but all there was around him to be found
Were the ravens of the elms, croaking their black, wicked sound.

"Victus, oh Victus! Savior of all that does exist!
Tell Odin your desire, and in fear do not resist.
You have spared his many people from certain pain and death
By being merciful to Fenrir and so ending his breath."

Victus spake, "I wish to go somewhere blood shall not flow;
A place to whence the eyes of Death dare never to follow.
Please grant me this one desire, oh Great God of the North.
Spare me the pains of seeing the face of Death henceforth!"

"As you have spoken, so then shall my word be upheld.
The ravens will guide you to where Death's thirst has been quelled.
So put away your blade and your twisted compass rose,
And we will take you to the place where Death's river never flows."

PART 4—CIRCE AND THE THREE DOORS OF TARTARUS

And upon the ravens' feathers poor Victus then did climb,
Going to where Death chose not to spend her evil time.
Higher they flew across land and ocean back to Greece
To a tiny little corner of the world where Death's works cease.

In that empty, desolate land where nothing lived or grew,
Death dared not to show her face, yet Dawn was hidden too.
The ravens stood by Victus, keeping out a watchful eye,
Unsure if this barren tract was where he'd meant to fly.

But Victus seemed content to stay upon the empty soil
In this place he need not fear to again with Death embroil—
No fearsome beasts or wicked gods to incite his wrath,
Only himself and the ravens who followed on his path.

But Victus soon would learn that all was not as he first thought
And he ventured forth to learn life may exist where Death is naught.
For this land of dust and twigs is a place of endless pain,
Inflicted without mercy as the wicked arbiter so deigns.

Pain of hunger, pain of thirst, doomed never to be sated.
A land of torment without death for those in life ill-fated.
Victus lifted his heavy eyes, fearing where he'd come
And saw the mighty Circe, though he knew not whence from.

"Victus, now before my eyes, of you much has been said:
The unnamed man by whom even gods are rendered dead."
Said Victus, "Tell me, oh Queen of Nymphs and Mighty Sorceress,
Am I where I fear to be? Is this land of Tartarus?"

(I)

Circe took him by hand and beckoned the ravens fore
And led them to the first of three, a roughly hewn stone door.
Upon the door in golden script the words were written thus:
Here Lies the Endless Fate of the Betrayer Prometheus.

Circe parted then her lips and sang a languid hymn.
The mighty door swung open, allowing passage there within.
Circe, being in this realm no more than a guide
Gently bowed her head to kiss his hand, then stood aside.

Victus and his ravens two then entered through the pass,
His feet now falling upon an endless, emerald field of grass.
He looked and saw not far off a single slab of stone
On which Prometheus was chained forever to atone

Victus drew his knife and stowed his twisted compass rose,
And as he warily approached, the Titan woke from a fitful doze.
Said he, "Put away your blade and kindly tell, what is your name?"
"I am Victus, who would know how to this fate you came."

The Titan answered, "I was tasked to cultivate the mortal race,
But in spite of my charge, I saw of them more than the base.
Defying my king's command, I gave to them the gift of fire,
And as such, a king-of-gods' eternal wrath I did acquire."

"So for my penance, here I must now be forever bound,
And each night for a feast, my flesh the eagles have found.
The agonizing pain is such that I wish to be dead,
Subsiding only when come the raptors to once more be fed."

Said Victus, "I can stay until the eagles shall descend,
And I will smite them to bring your tortured bondage to an end.
For neither from the gods nor from a great wolf did I shy.
Gladly will I bloody my knife to let your torment die!"

"Victus, Victus, with your heroic heart so good and true,
What you lack in name and blood is gained by such virtue.
But Tartarus is well beyond even your fearless hand,
For Death has no presence here in this pitiful land."

"Return with the ravens now to your guide at the door
And dwell upon my eternal sufferings no more.
There remains much more that your eyes have still yet to see,
For this is but the first door of the Tartarus three."

Victus sheathed his blade and turned, mournful in defeat,
Fearful to think what behind the other doors he would soon meet.
Upon returning, he found fair Circe waiting for him there
And asked of her any wisdom or council she might share.

Touching his cheek then with an apologetic caress,
She wished for a way to spare him further duress,
But led ravens and him forth to the next standing door,
All knowing that each step would but fracture his spirit more.

"No," spoke Victus, thus refusing to be sent so away.
"I shan't so easily depart in failure on this day.
Ravens of Odin, god of the north in strength and might,
You shall guard Prometheus from the raptors day and night."

"If we may not slay the fowl or break eternal bind,
We'll do what we can to show the mercy of mortalkind.
So now depart from me and fly to greater upright task
And further requests of you I shall no longer ask."

So off they flew back through the door to be the Titan's guard,
Taking up the post to the god-king's verdict disregard.
And Victus turned and walked away, on his own once more,
And was greeted by Circe, still waiting for him at the door.

(II)

Circe took Victus by the hand and beckoned him once more
And led him to the next of three, a great, carved oaken door.
Upon the door in golden script, words were written thus:
Behold the Endless Fate of the Murderer Tantalus

Circe again parted her lips to sing the languid hymn.
The mighty door swung open, allowing passage there within.
Circe, being in this realm no more than a guide,
Gently bowed her head to kiss his hand, then stood aside.

Victus stepped across yet another enchanted entryway,
Wondering what wicked game the Fates chose here to play.
Trusting what the fire god spake, he sheathed now his blade
And walked forth in fear of the debt he would see being paid.

Over fruitful hills and rolling streams he there traversed
And wondered what could be such that this place was so accursed?
The trees were many, branches full of fruit all ripe and red.
The water flowed so cold and clear—what could be here to dread?

Then there ahead, he saw an old man sitting in the shade,
And Victus wondered for what crimes his punishment was paid.
The man sat staring, overcome as if with heavy gloom.
Victus then approached and said, "Tantalus, I presume?"

"You must be Victus, the slayer of Olympus' haughty seats.
Welcome to the place where grow the sweetest fruits none eats.
Where is water clean and clear, yet never soothed is thirst—
A more torturous fate upon a mortal no god has ever cursed.

"For upon approach, the waters shall only recede,
And the fruits rise ever higher when try you to sate thy need.
So here I sit to gaze upon the best of Demeter's hand,
Never able to quench or taste that which enriches this land."

Victus heard the sorrowful words of this long-broken man
And asked of the events for which this torment first began.
Tantalus looked to Victus as tears fell down his face
And with much courage, revealed to this foreigner his disgrace.

"A friend of the Olympians was I for many faithful years,
Counted by the king of the gods an equal to his peers.
But wickedness filled my heart, and sins I did commit:
Ambrosia and secrets of the gods, I sold for my profit.

"But worse than all this was my final act of heinous sin,
For I slew mine own son, and to the gods I served his skin.
Death is the only justice that I now wish they would serve,
But the king felt death more merciful than that which I deserve.

"So here I sit, condemned to dwell on my crimes, never dying,
Reflecting on my filicide, my greed, and all my lying.
Visions of my wickedness ever dancing in my eyes,
All for the spite that consumes the king, god of the skies."

Victus rose to stand and spoke to this man from his heart:
"Death may not be possible, but I shan't be told hope hath no part.
Drink is your desire, and so drink I shall hence to you give,
For within my blood does the power of the great wolf Fenrir live.

"A beast of honor who, with selfless courage and sacrifice,
Gave to me a drop of his own blood as he paid his final price.
So I draw this blade that has felled both god and beast
And draw red Nordic blood on which for you to finally feast.

"Quench from mortal vein your thirst and hunger here no longer,
And to the bastard king, prove once and all that Tantalus is stronger.
See now the beauty of this realm and ease at last your spirit.
In forgiveness peace is found, and none should ever fear it."

Victus drew the blade across his flesh; drew blood imbued.
Tantalus drank then from his vein and felt at once renewed,
Light returning to his eyes and rose upon his cheek,
As he found here in Victus what for aeons he did seek.

Tantalus stood and grabbed Victus close beneath the spreading tree,
Giving him the strong embrace of a man at last set free.
Together did they walk, approaching the great wooden door,
And Victus passed through, knowing there still remained one more.

He reached the pass where Circe stood, waiting for him there,
And marked the change and feel of the empty, barren air.
He desired not to cross the next threshold and more pain see,
But Victus went forth knowing after two must next come three.

(III)

Circe took him by hand and beckoned him once more
And led them to the last of three: a thick black iron door.
Upon the door in golden script the words were written thus:
Here Find the Endless Fate of the Deceiver Sisyphus

Circe for the final time sang her languid, mournful hymn.
The dreadful door swung open, allowing passage there within.
Then Circe, being in this realm no more than a guide,
Gently bowed her head to kiss his hand, then stood aside.

As twice before now Victus passed, this time through iron gate,
The weariness in his bones so heavy as to be a weight.
But on he pressed to see this last and final trial through
In hopes that soon thereafter he could leave this land for true.

He wound his way then through a dry and rocky valley pass,
Where brown-veined boulders lined the landscape of his new trespass.
Long he wandered the desolate realm in the only possible direction
To find what poor fool was here, and under what tortured subjection.

The path slowly grew wider as he came upon a hill,
Whereupon he found an old man who briefly stood still.
Then, with strength beyond his years, a boulder there he pressed
Up toward the peak, never stopping once for breath or rest.

Yet, just as the man and his burden came upon their goal,
He lost his strength and footing, and so, down did the boulder roll.
As the stone came to a stop below, the man broke down to weep,
His old eyes full of sorrow and the tracks of his tears carved deep.

Down the hill the man then walked at a slow and mournful pace,
Long years of brutal labor etched into his ancient face.
Victus neared him now as he leaned upon the boulder again,
Cautious, as despite his age, the man held much strength within.

Victus spoke with gentle voice to catch the old man's eye.
"Sir, please rest a moment—allow your tears and sweat to dry.
I am Victus, of no pure blood, born of hate and shame.
I ask you with reverent respect, may I know your name?"

The man then turned his face and, gazing upon Victus,
Told him, "My name matters not, but I once was called Sisyphus,
The high king of Ephyra, a bountiful, wealthy state,
But through deceit and prideful greed did I earn this fate.

"I deceived the god-king, and so into the Unseen was I cast,
Where my repentance and remorse grew bountiful and fast.
Hades spoke in my defense, but the king's pride was wounded still.
And so, the king slandered his own blood and placed me on this hill.

"To gods and mortals, he denounced Hades as a greedy lord of death,
And so rendered him reviled by all those who still draw breath.
So we both have been slighted by the god-king of the skies,
But it's the libel against Hades that bring tears still to my eyes.

"My punishment upon this hill is the making of my own,
And through eternal labor I hope to perhaps someday atone.
To roll this stone up to the top and find my final rest,
But Zeus brings bitter failure at the last; his endless jest."

In hearing these chronicles, the wrath of Victus burned,
Hating more this royal god with ev'ry tale he learned.
"Your punishment is wholly unjust for crimes long in the past.
I swear to you, Sisyphus, you've pushed this boulder for the last!"

Victus neared the stone and took the knife out from his belt,
Resolving to clear Sisyphus of the fate unjustly dealt.
Next removed he then the precious, twisted compass rose,
His one cherished possession, now for justice to dispose.

Using the blade soaked with blood of god and beast alike,
He rent the twisted compass rose with a single strike.
Victus took the blade and drew blood from each of his palms,
Allowing it to flow upon the rose in propitious red alms.

Setting then the first of two upon the boulder of cruel jest,
The next he set upon the unattained place of final rest.
Sisyphus there stood, watching with wild-eyed disbelief,
Seeing untold magics that here and now gave him relief.

This daunting hill that for so long had stood so steep and high,
Like a lioness by a pond then lowered its haunches down to lie.
And the boulder of torment, imbued with blood and rose,
Rolled of its own accord to bring his torture to a close.

 pieces met, and there forth threw a great, thunderous sound
As the boulder shattered and became naught but dust upon the ground.
Sisyphus fell to his knees and wept with a grateful cry,
No longer punished beneath the heel of the god of the sky.

Sisyphus then embraced Victus and thanked him once more,
Hesitant for him to take his leave through the black iron door.
But knowing his departure was what fate would decree,
Victus turned and ventured back to the patient, fair Circe.

There she stood, waiting still in all her radiant splendor,
And she took his wounded hand, compassionate and tender.
Walking forth together into the dim of shadowed Tartarus,
There came thunder from the skies in hateful shout: "Victus!"

PART 5—THE MEETING OF ZEUS

Victus and Circe stopped then where they stood upon the path,
Both knowing without question the source of this vicious wrath.
Of the works of Victus, the king of the gods was made aware,
And great Zeus had now come forth, his reputation to repair.

Victus, man of honor, stood between Zeus and the girl,
As the clouds and wind about them both began to scream and swirl.
But Victus, from his stance, was neither shaken nor moved,
For a man without a home is not so easily removed.

The king of the gods still had yet more power to display,
As he called forth the lightning from the clouds dark and gray.
But Victus stood there, tall, and broke not his burning stare,
For this mortal was not one to shy away from such a dare.

Then the vengeful king did finally speak aloud with thunder:
"Behind what fool does fair Circe hide, I am left to wonder?
Fool to think he can undo all judgments I decreed
And make they who fall under my divine bonds to be freed?

"Stand not as a coward and tell me now of your name,
That I may know who will be ever here enshrined in shame.
Be gone now, Circe, for you have no more part to play here,
For I find this boy now worthy to learn of righteous fear."

As Victus turned to her, Circe held out her warm hand to he
And vanished then, no longer guide and guard of the doors three.
And so there stood the greatest god who sat upon Olympus,
Naught more left in this realm but mighty Zeus and poor Victus.

Victus turned then back to face the wicked godly king
With full understanding of the wrath Zeus soon would bring.
Removing then his knife that slew both god and beast alike,
While all about him Zeus brought forth another lightning strike.

"My name is but Victus, and none is more thereafter to be said.
Since my day of birth, I have been worth less alive than dead.
But in my traveled days, I have slain both god and beast,
While you do nothing but upon the pain of mortals feast.

"So gather now your thunder and cast forth all your lightning—
Call up all your power that every mortal finds so frightening.
Strain to evoke my terror with all your divine might,
But I shall stand here, foolish, prepared to die in this fight."

The great king Zeus struck hard, moving as swift as the storm
As rain and hail fell about them like a vile demon swarm.
Victus, though, was cunning, and countered with his trusted blade,
But with flesh like forged iron was the king of the gods so made.

His knife making no puncture and the god's skin with no split,
Victus knew his life was lost, but still refused to quit.
Not yet willing to concede, or lay down here just to die,
He rallied then and pushed his blade straight into the god's eye.

Zeus, he then did utter forth a fearful blood-soaked shout,
And in the god-king's voice, one could hear a twinge of doubt.
Victus then moved quickly for yet more pain to introduce
And plucked forth from his bloody head the other eye of Zeus.

Blind with more than rage, Zeus stuck with a tremendous bolt,
Hoping to end Victus and his insolent revolt.
But Victus, having nothing left of this mortal life to lose,
No loving family, close companion, nor insightful muse,

Did again so rise with his blade clutched in his fist
And charged at Zeus, determined this be the last day he exist.
But Zeus called up the mist and clouds from the eternal skies
And saw every move that Victus made as if with his own eyes.

He felt each step and every turn that the mortal warrior made
And listened to the wind that sang against his blasphemous blade.
As he felt Victus draw nearer, the god began to gloat
And in his hate and malice took hold of Victus by the throat.

Gripping tight the mortal throat, Zeus held Victus' face near,
And so, whispered just loud enough that the warrior could hear:
"You have done great works that some may honor and call brave,
But for your efforts you shall find here nothing more than a grave.

"Die now in manner neither great nor honorable nor grand—
Die now, Victus, here in the palm of mine own mighty hand.
As I feel the life leave you, oh how I wish I could see,
To know the look in your eyes as your last living moments flee."

The king of gods lifted then the mortal man and held him thus,
And with final, crushing strength drew the last breath of Victus.
Dropping then his lifeless body to the ground at his feet,
Zeus stood and relished, smiling, his vengeance now complete.

And so, here the lifeless and cold body of Victus lies
On the desolate plains of Tartarus, beneath the sunless skies.
But all was not yet finished for the wicked lightning king,
For the bells of greater vengeance were soon forth to ring.

PART 6—THE NEW DAWN

Zeus stands in triumph as a rumble is felt from within the ground,
Accompanied by such a harsh and fearful growling sound.
Circe breaks now from the clouds, driving a chariot of light,
And with her divine power, returns to Zeus his sight.

"Have sight again, oh king, for your death now draws near you,
As all have gathered to collect on the debts which they are due.
See Hades rise, the brother persecuted by your slander,
Sworn as he stands here to be your final day's Lysander."

"See Prometheus, Tantalus, Sisyphus as well—
Watch as Fenrir awakens by my own arcane spell.
Halcyon and Cassiopeia are joined together in our cause;
Odin and his ravens no longer concerned with your laws.

"We fight now to break free from beneath your wicked heel
And avenge mighty Victus, whose life you did cruelly steal.
For he was a man of honor, upright of noble heart,
And it is in his name our fear of you now sees fit to depart.

"Charon stands aside as the tortured souls in his charge rise,
Joining all those gathered to ensure the hateful god now dies.
The chains that held Prometheus shall your body now keep still,
As Fenrir prepares on your flesh to forever feast at will.

"Halcyon, Cassiopeia, and Odin now bear witness,
As desire for revenge within us all grows restless.
I draw now my sword as you look fixed upon my eyes
And see that it's by Circe's hand that you, oh king, now die."

As Circe spake, she took hold of Zeus by his long hair of gray
And drew her sword across his throat, and thus the king did slay.
There fell then the wicked Zeus, god of nothing, king no more,
For a time of peace and wisdom is what now is in store.

Hades approached and spoke in calm of the momentous hour:
"Hail to Circe, and to her great queenly courage and power!
She shall sit upon Olympus, enthroned so to by all be seen,
Seated ever at the right hand of our new wise queen!"

As Hades spoke there from the skies did then descend a sound,
Gentle and melodic to announce the queen now crowned.
All fell then upon their knees amid the swelling ocarina,
As walked now before them the newly crowned queen Athena.

"None shall kneel before me upon this breaking of new dawn,
For days of subjugation in the realm have now passed on.
And in this moment, many greater acts do lay before us,
For first we must make proper memorial to the fallen Victus.

"To Odin we give the knife that Victus did so bravely wield,
Which to he and his people shall become a lasting shield—
Giving freedom to Fenrir from fate and caged dwelling,
Sparing the destruction of Ragnarok's foretelling.

"The compass rose, rent asunder, to Hades it shall go,
To guide the spirits of the fallen and the right path to them show.
And a tomb shall be made at the very peak of high Olympus
Thus, to watch over all in death shall be the honored Victus.

"As none again shall be greater than this mortal of no name,
For by his courageous heart, this realm will never be the same.
So to remember he and his chronicles we must,
Upon the name Victus does Olympus swear to be just.

"Circe, I now ask you to gather Victus to your chest
And carry him now to where he shall find eternal rest.
Your power and courage are like none ever seen before,
So I beg to trespass upon your strength now once more.

"Lay brave Victus in his tomb at high Olympus' peak.
Let his name be a beacon for all them who are weak.
Showing there are no chains which one can never escape—
That they may always know their fate is their own to shape."

Circe bowed then reverently, as did all within the throng,
And holding Victus, she sang out in Tartarus her final song.
"As the Goddess and Queen desires, so then shall I serve
To escort mighty Victus to the seat he does deserve.

"He gave his life to make right many old, dishonored sins.
From his sacrifice, a new dawn of the realms begins.
From the fields of Valhalla to the mountain of the gods,
No longer will mortal and deity be at eternal odds."

Circe then got to her feet to take her solemn leave from this place,
As all present took to their knees and let tears flow down their face.
Fenrir bowed to Odin, grateful once again to stand.
And in his jaws took the corpse of Zeus, fading from this land.

Odin held the blade of mighty Victus and sheathed it so.
Then to Asgard with his ravens did he silently go.
Hades gathered up the two twisted compass halves
And left to place them both along the dark underworld paths.

The Queen turned to all those remaining whom Victus had freed
And charged for their last of penance but one final deed:
To command the birds and the stars and all that they shall meet
To sing the Lament of Victus and recount his greatest feat.

A LIGHT WITHIN THE NIGHTMARES

PART 1—UPON THE MEETING BY THE BIRCH

PART 2—OF ELVES AND MIS-UNDERSTANDINGS

PART 3—A CAVE FOR CAUCHEMAR'S CURSE

PART 4—THE DESTRUCTION OF PALAIS DES RÊVES

PART 5—THE RISING OF A KING

PART 6—THE CROWNING OF ALIENORPART 7—WAR

PART 8—THE BRAVE GIRL, THE QUEEN, THE ELF, THE SORCERER, AND THE DRAGON

PART 9—DEPARTING FROM PALAIS DES RÊVES

PART 1—UPON THE MEETING BY THE BIRCH

Alienor woke in the night as a great storm thrashed about.
The wind howled as the clouds gave a thundering shout.
She went to her window to watch the sky show its might,
But out beneath the old birch she saw a shape in the night.

She showed no fear as she ran into the raging storm,
For she was intrigued by what cast the shadowy form.
How could such a small girl come to be so very brave,
Fearing not the storm, nor shadow, nor risk of the grave?

Out across the clearing and the fast-rising stream,
As if lost in a trance or a childhood dream,
She drew closer to what cast the intriguing shade,
And when the lightning flashed, she still was not afraid.

There looming before Alienor stood a formidable beast,
A hulking figure, standing thrice her size at the least.
The beast turned its great head to reveal a skull full of horns,
Growling to show a mouth full of fangs like long thorns.

Clad in scales of smooth gray streaked with deep ruby red,
Its slit-pupiled eyes glowed brightest green with dread.
Down its sinuous back grew a long, coarse amber mane,
And Alienor simply stood before this beast in the rain.

She looked on it softly as it made a horrible sound,
Showing a gentle smile to the beast that she had found.
Gazing at the creature as it growled to evoke her fear,
All Alienor felt in her heart was delight and good cheer.

She sat upon the ground and stared at the beast as it roared,
And looming thus, it marveled at these actions so untoward.
It knelt down beside her on the rain-soaked, grassy land,
And then Alienor reached out and offered it her hand.

"You need not to be afraid, or to give such a great shout."
The little girl's voice rang like a song without a doubt.
So the beast then took a seat and took Alienor's palm,
And for the first this night, all around the two was calm.

"Can you understand me and all the words I speak?
Do you find yourself lost, or is this the place you seek?"
The beast sat there a moment, looking at the girl so frail
And then opened his mouth to tell Alienor his tale.

"This foreign realm is indeed not where I am meant to be.
From a sorcerer of my own world was I forced to flee.
Using the magic I possess to escape from his claim,
I have fled for my life, and to this frightful place I came."

"I am a creature of magic, and desire only peace—
A place to live without fear, where my hiding can cease.
But from what little I have seen of this land in the east,
I fear there is no place here for this vagabond beast."

Alienor looked on the creature with sadness in her eyes
And with determined courage then to her feet did rise.
"I promise from me you have naught but kindness in store.
Now rise, my new friend, and you may call me Alienor."

"You are correct, sir, for this meadow indeed is not secure,
But I will join you to find a place where your safety is sure.
So come, let us be off, for soon the dawn will arise,
And those of the village will look on you with fearful eyes."

The beast arose, and upon his shoulder there sat Alienor,
And they walked until they saw the spreading birch no more.
North to the hills between Harlech and Corris they walked
Through thick forests to ensure all sight of them was blocked.

"May I ask thee a question, my dear Alienor?
And please, my little friend, do call me Cauchemar."
"Ask any question you wish, Cauchemar, my new friend.
I will give you any knowledge I have to extend."

"What made you come to me in the thundering of the night,
And how is it I failed to conjure within you any fright?
Do you possess a great magic uncommonly found,
Such that you saw my need in spite of my threatening sound?"

"Cauchemar, I must tell you, no magic does here live,
And if I possessed any, it to you I would gladly give.
My years may be few, but still true pain I have seen,
And pain I saw when the lightning showed your sad eyes of green."

Cauchemar then stopped and set Alienor down on her feet,
And kneeling down low so that their eyes could firmly meet,
He there pushed his long claws deep into the rich ground
And spoke low words while a light, glowing green, gathered round.

"Open wide your eyes, Alienor, and look all about.
See now what lies hidden from others by their fear and doubt.
I offer you the magic beneath my scales of red and gray—
Magic to remain yours even should our paths part way."

"Listen well, good Alienor, to all you now can hear:
The speech of fowl and beast shall to you ring loud and clear.
The ancient magic of Cauchemar in this realm now awakes,
And now the laws of your world are beneath you to break."

As the light began to fade and Cauchemar then rose,
Alienor heard many sounds as her eyes drifted closed.
Voices of the vast forest from all points around,
Of the birds and wolves and creatures who dwelt underground.

She opened wide her eyes to see many miles ahead,
And seeing through even darkened thicket, Alienor then said,
"Cauchemar, why do you give to me such a mighty favor?"
"'Tis but a little gift to thank my courageous savior."

And so, continue on they did, the beast and girl, yet more
Through the deep, dark forest to where the hilltops rise and soar.
Friends they soon became, in spite of all universal walls,
All because one brave little girl answered a monster's calls.

PART 2—OF ELVES AND MISUNDERSTANDINGS

As they traveled through the passage of the rolling hills,
They rested in a clearing filled with tulips and cranebills.
Using her new gift, young Alienor looked far ahead,
And in tones of grave concern to Cauchemar then said,

"Cauchemar, the creatures of the forest have begun to flee in fear,
But the cause of all their terror I can neither see nor hear.
For weeks the beasts and I have spoken in peaceful accord.
Does something full of wickedness now this way come toward?

"For at first, they were cautious of thee, gentle Cauchemar.
But we spoke, and they now know of how good and kind you are.
What would cause such panic in both predator and prey
That neither would feel safe to within their own home stay?"

Cauchemar stopped to kneel and put his face to the ground,
His green eyes shining as he listened to the earth's secret sound.
Quickly then he rose and placed Alienor on his shoulder
As they both felt the warm summer wind turn suddenly colder.

Cauchemar ran swiftly, carrying the brave young girl
As all about the sky grew dark, and the wind began to swirl.
The lightning flashed before them, striking out to split an oak,
And there before them in the thunder stood a figure 'neath a cloak.

The foreboding figure looked upon them with eyes of icy blue,
And slowly forth from his side, a shimmering sword he drew.
Leveling it thus at the two companions, he then spoke
As he revealed his face from beneath the deep hood of his cloak.

The Song of Circe and Other Simple Musings

"You are not welcome here, horrid beast of foreign land.
On behalf of all the elves, I levy this command:
Do not make me draw thy blood and stain this peaceful place.
This one chance to flee will be thy only offered grace."

Alienor then leapt down from her perch and strode ahead,
And with much anger and authority, she then bravely said,
"Who art thou to speak to Cauchemar in such foul words,
When his genteel nature is known even by the birds?

"He seeks only shelter as refugee from his own realm,
And we wish only safe passage through this host of elm.
So put away your sword and your vile, ignorant tongue,
And call forth to the light they who sit hidden among."

The elven guardsman paused, then offered a wry smile to Alienor,
And with a whistle, called then forth a great number more.
A gathering of ancient elves formed around them there,
But into the distance did Alienor level her stern stare.

As the many elves surrounded both the girl and beast,
Their disdain for the travelers was only twofold increased
But what they did not foresee was the cunning of Alienor,
As she called to the wolves who gathered soon in numbers more.

Wolves from all around the wood did come to obey Alienor's call,
And thus undid the hostile threat of this elven shield wall.
The elves saw that they could not against so many stand and fight,
So they lay down their arms with empty hands in Alienor's sight.

Alienor approached the captain, never once showing fear,
And spoke her next words clearly for all present to hear:
"Who are you vicious lot to draw swords upon we two?
Travelers as we are, who are merely passing through.

"Stand and speak like a man, or do you fear I, a girl?
Let your secrets spill before me and in truth unfurl!"
The captain of the elves gazed long upon young Alienor
And, showing honor, knelt there then upon the forest floor.

"My name is Forêt, captain of the woodland guards you see.
We are charged to protect the forest—every creature and tree—
Staying hidden from mortal sight, unless great is our need,
To which we hesitate not to make the interloper bleed.

"Tell me who in truth thou art, for a simple girl you cannot be.
Is this beast under your command, as the wolves seem to be?
Speak well, little one, for we will know if thou doth lie.
On my knee I speak to you with honor in my eye."

Alienor looked on Forêt with pity in her heart,
Knowing from ignorance did these violent actions start.
"Listen to the wolves, and they'll tell all you need to know.
A simple girl am I who befriended Cauchemar in his woe."

Alienor then called forth one of the wolves to her side,
And the wolf spoke to Forêt and her account he testified.
Upon hearing the tale of these friends, the assembled elves did weep
And swore their secrets and their safety the elves would ever keep.

The Song of Circe and Other Simple Musings

Forêt rose and to Cauchemar he spoke with humble words,
As Alienor dismissed the wolves from the gathered hoards.
Forêt bowed before Cauchemar and offered him a gift:
From within the folds of his long cloak, a fine dagger did he lift.

"Your gift is kind, Forêt Elf, but I fear I cannot accept.
Far more use would this knife be if by Alienor it was kept.
For her wisdom and her kindness exceeds any I have known,
As even unto you gathered it was mercy that was shown"

Forêt turned to face where Alienor did firmly stand
And knelt before the courageous girl and took her gentle hand.
"This dagger is far more than a simple sharp steel blade.
Forged within are many spells that the ancient elves made."

"It can serve as light in darkness, when all hope feels lost,
Or kindle for thee a fire to halt all-consuming frost.
And if still more for you is needed than simple light and flame,
Place the dagger on a tree's root and whisper my name.

"And I, along with every elf who dwells in this vast land
Will take up arms to assist at your brave little hand.
For you, Alienor, are far greater than all the rest,
And within these woods you both shall ever be our guest."

PART 3—A CAVE FOR CAUCHEMAR'S CURSE

Alienor woke once again to the terrified sound
Of her dear friend Cauchemar thrashing on the ground,
Screaming as he fought the many demons of his dreams
While Alienor tried to wake Cauchemar from his screams.

Finally, Cauchemar did wake from his nocturnal fright
As Alienor held him in her arms, comfortingly close and tight.
"It seems to me your nightmares grow worse by the evening.
We must soon find a remedy for your nightly grieving.

"I sent ravens to speak with Forêt, seeking his advice.
In reply, he sent visions of forests hidden 'neath mountainous ice.
He showed to me vast caves where deep magic does yet thrive—
A great magic that, in spite of its age, today does still survive."

"What have we to lose if we alter our present course
So we may seek relief for you in this magical source?
Let us make for the northern caves of the Cairngorms' peaks
To meet the faerie clan who lives there and with their leader speak."

Northward through the snow did Alienor and Cauchemar pace
As Alienor called upon the rooks to be their guides to this place.
After many long miles, weary both in body and in mind,
The cave of faeries did the travelers at long last come to find.

But the great entrance was barren and covered up with snow,
And within this cave there was not the slightest light to show.
In Cauchemar's green eyes was a deep, hollow sadness wrought
At finding naught but darkness in place of the magic he had sought.

He fell upon his knees where the entrance should be kept
And, with his horned head in clawed hands, there shamelessly wept.
How far had he come at the prospect of peace and rest,
Choosing the frost of the north over the shores of the west?

But Alienor, being just as clever as she was brave
Then drew forth the dagger-gift that Forêt to her gave.
Closing her eyes, wanting only to ease her friend's hurt,
She thrust the dagger's blade hard into the black, frozen dirt.

Deep thunder seemed to peal from within the spell-forged blade
As light spidered out from it across the frosted, lifeless grade.
The hilt, then glowing with a blue and green pulsating light,
Shone then forth, bringing a lush landscape into sight.

Cauchemar and Alienor stood together hand in hand
As before their eyes grew the most green and fertile land.
"This magic is old and strong," did Cauchemar then speak,
"To make even one such as I in its presence seem to be weak."

"Cauchemar, dear friend from another realm so far away,
I will not permit such unkind things about yourself for you to say.
For you've strength within your spirit all can plainly see—
Strength so abundant that even some you have shared with me.

"Come now, Cauchemar, and into this cave we now go,
For the magic beckons stronger as the plants still grow.
Let us find the queen of faeries that in this land does dwell
So she can lift from your mind this horrid nightmare spell."

Forward they together walked into the forest sprung from stone,
Seeking to find the faerie queen and fall before her throne
To plead for magic and mercy to ease Cauchemar's violent sleep
And sow for him new fields of rest, ripe for his dreams to reap.

"Welcome, travelers, to my home here beneath the frost,
Where magical entry absolves those welcome of any due cost.
Address me as Titania, which is my given name.
Enter here as friends to I, and we shall treat you as the same."

There before the two companions the great faerie queen stood,
Shining from her all the light that filled the enchanted wood.
Her face was full of beauty unlike any prior known,
And strength and power to match it all about her shone.

The friends began to kneel, but Titania bid them rise
And fixed her bright gaze firmly upon the travelers' eyes.
"None shall so kneel within this realm of magic and pure light,
For to breach the veil means your intents are proven just and right.

"The roots of this forest have forespoken of your woes,
But the true torment of Cauchemar, no one here yet knows.
I see the pain you try to hide in your gentle green eyes,
And tear stains upon your cheeks betray your smiling lies.

"Alienor's concern for you runs deep within her soul,
As she knows not for you how to comfort or console.
She cares more for you above all else to ever exist,
And so, her quest for your peace does constantly persist.

"So lower now your kindly head, gray-scaled and many-horned,
Crowned with spikes though you deny the purpose which adorned.
We faeries have a sight beyond the realm within this cave,
And we have seen the land you fought so desperately to save."

Cauchemar took the queen's soft hands, tears flowing down his face
As he recalled the dark destruction that so recently took place.
Brave Alienor then placed her own small hands upon theirs as well
And saw for herself the vision of how Cauchemar's homeland fell.

PART 4—THE DESTRUCTION OF PALAIS DES RÊVES

The party camped near the castle of black stone in fright.
To broker of peace, Cauchemar met with Deamhan the White,
A mighty sorcerer with long hair the color of snow.
Cauchemar pleaded to Deamhan for mercy to show.

"Cauchemar the king comes now to bow before my feet
In hopes that at my table I would offer to him seat.
Art thou not embarrassed to prostrate yourself low,
Or is your weakness greater than even I would know?"

Cauchemar indeed was the peaceful king of all his race,
Creatures who for ages lived in peace within this place,
Creating the kingdom known to all as Palais des Rêves,
Where magic maintained peace for all that there did live.

Cauchemar knew this effort would most like be in vain,
But better he be mocked than all his kingdom to be slain.
"We would annex to you a great portion of our land.
All we ask is for you to stay your destructive hand.

"We keep well to ourselves and wish only for peace.
We beg you to call back your ranks so the fighting may cease.
Though we wish never to lift arms or to display our might,
Should they rise, be warned: we will stand and fight."

Deamhan rose and looked hard into Cauchemar's green eyes,
Knowing this king of beasts before him never spoke in lies.
"Get from my sight and return to your camp upon the plains.
My patience for your arrogance now quickly wanes.

"By sundown tomorrow my response will be made.
Now begone from here, else my generosity fade."
So Cauchemar turned away and left that wicked place,
Not knowing yet the final fate of himself or of his race.

The next day, before the sun could make its downward fall,
Cauchemar gathered his people, such to speak before them all.
But as he began, there came a black mist from the ground,
And forth from it was uttered a bloodcurdling sound.

The voice of Deamhan the White echoed out across the field
As he launched an attack from which there could be no shield.
Cauchemar watched, helpless, as the mist engulfed all of his kind,
And one by one he poisoned them, breaking each one's mind.

Cauchemar stood helpless while his small kingdom fell prey,
As the screams of his people echoed, ghastly and fey.
They fell upon the ground and writhed in tears before his feet,
And Cauchemar then felt an approaching wave of heat.

Fire rose around him as the black mist became flame,
And all those who were tortured cried out Cauchemar's name.
The screaming faded soon enough. Ash was all left to be found,
But Cauchemar's heart could not be rid of the echoing sound.

Falling to his knees, he wept, clawing at the ashen dirt,
Broken that one wicked man could inflict so much hurt.
From the black mist rose the figure of Deamhan the White
As Cauchemar cowered, overcome with awful fright.

"I care not for your land or your so-called peaceful accord,
I only wish to see your foul kind come to their just reward.
So behold once more as I make my power well seen.
Gaze upon my final word with your weak eyes of green!"

There then came before Cauchemar, bound by the black mist,
The pinnacle of the hate Deamhan held in his fist:
Cauchemar's wife and children set for him to see,
And Deamhan took their lives, without care for his plea.

Cauchemar stood and ran to the now ashen pile,
Wailing and cursing Deamhan in hatred all the while.
But the mist rose once again, and so Cauchemar fled
And used what magic he had left to hide from Deamhan's dread.

At the flash of light when from his realm he did depart,
Alienor and Titania did see this journey's start.
Breaking their hold, Cauchemar fell to his knees in tears,
And all within the faeries' cave understood his fears.

PART 5—THE RISING OF A KING

Cauchemar wept loud and long without any care of witness
As he lay in Alienor's arms, heartbroken and listless.
After many long and painful moments had gone past,
Cauchemar gathered himself up to address them all at last.

"Forgive my lack of composure before you all gathered here,
But even this does give full measure to my ever-present fear.
It shows not the gravity of the ways in which I failed,
For you know not the reason that I am horned and scaled.

"I was called by my kind to be a leader for them there,
And so proved myself wise and strong, yet still full of care.
So, in a ceremony before an ancient wall of stone,
The magic of my people was called forth and made my own.

"These horns grew from my head when I was thereby anointed,
And armored in these colored scales when my position was appointed.
My charge was to protect and judge, seeking only peace,
And to use wisdom to ensure all threats to my race to decrease.

"But Deamhan was more wicked than any king could fathom,
And he created within my world a bottomless black chasm.
His threats against my race were relentless and without end,
And it fell upon myself each time to protect and defend.

"But in the end, he took from me all I ever held within my hands,
Sowing blood and murder all across our boundless lands!
And when time came for me to stand for all that was good and just,
He tore my spirit from me, leaving only ash and dust!

"While I am a creature of magic, and I keep to peaceful ways,
My greatest wish is to see a time when for his crimes he pays.
I no longer care for peace, nor will I accept his penance,
For should I lay eyes on Deamhan, I will seek my vengeance!"

As Cauchemar spoke, he stood taller in growing power and might
As from his fists green flame erupted with immense, blinding light.
Alienor then smiled, seeing the new face of her friend
As he cast aside the fear under which he long did bend.

Titania beamed to see the new turning of this great beast
And sent forth a brilliant light to the forests of the east.
"Come ye forth, all you fierce creatures of forest and night!
Gather and prepare now for this great mystical fight!"

The ravens called and flocked in the sky like a black sheet
As wolves and stags emerged to bow before Titania's feet.
And at the entrance of the enchanted cave, they saw did stand
Mighty Forêt with all the elven warriors of the land,

Each standing ready in armor of shining gold and black,
With cloaks of ornate embroidery draped across their backs.
Perfect ranks as far back into the woods as could be seen,
And Forêt bowed before Titania and addressed, "My Queen."

From the shadowed trees of Titania's realm did then appear
The faerie army clad in mail, wielding broad-tipped spears.
Lastly then did Alienor approach Cauchemar the Great
And, drawing forth her dagger, said, "Let this be our fate!"

PART 6—THE CROWNING OF ALIENOR

Titania approached brave Alienor as she there stood tall
And smiled as she knelt before her in the view of all.
In the queen's outstretched hand did a crown of laurels form,
For Alienor's bravery would be the beacon of this storm.

"None who dwell here in this realm, or others that remain unseen,
Have ever been so welcomed by elves or fairy queen.
Alienor is bravest and most compassionate of all,
For when all else showed fear, she answered Cauchemar's call."

"Upon her shoulders she carries now the weight of all our lands,
Choosing always justice when others would take a coward's stand.
I crown her now as regent of the nations gathered here,
For she will lead us forth to battle, whatsoever we all fear.

"For what is to stop Deamhan from breaking through this veil
And weaving through even our realm a bloody, tear-stained trail?
So we choose to fight, and not just for Cauchemar's peace.
We fight so the coming darkness will, before it descends, cease.

"As I crown brave Alienor in the sight of all you now,
We here assembled shall before this mighty, brave girl bow.
For she so chose to rescue Cauchemar beneath the birch that night
And stands here with us all, ready and willing now to fight!"

As the laurels lay upon Alienor's long amber hair,
All those in her assembly knelt to pledge allegiance there.
Forêt then rose and strode to meet with Alienor the Brave,
And a new gift from the realm of elves Forêt proudly gave.

"Though you stand no taller than any gathered here about,
Of our faith in you, bold Alienor, there can be no doubt.
From the elven crown we offer you this spell-forged sword
And its scabbard of gold and leather in which is stored.

"As it is long and broad, the blade shall never show spot of rust,
And its ensorcelled metal weighs no more than a mote of dust.
No higher gift can come from the great nation of the elves,
And with this we bind and pledge to you all of ourselves."

Cauchemar, then standing taller still than even before,
Said, "Many words have been spoken, but if I may add more:
I shan't ask you to stand down or say this fight is my own,
For Deamhan will not cease until each realm is of bone.

"Yes, I cowered once in fear at the wrath he did enact.
Of my sad failures and sins, I will not here detract.
But I pledge not for Forêt or to Titania the queen,
But to my great friend, Alienor, the bravest ever seen."

"As I wished only to hide from the death of all my kind,
A little girl braved the tempest, and there did she find
A king who had forgotten who he once was before,
And now, in her hallowed name, peace we fight to restore!

"In the name of brave Alienor, I swear now before all:
Neither will my courage ever again falter or fall.
I will give my last breath to end Deamhan's evil reign.
Upon my life, peace from his grip we shall now regain!"

And as all cheered within the enchanted faeries' land,
Titania, Forêt, and Cauchemar joined together hand in hand.
At the mouth of the cave where the frost met with the trees,
A gateway opened, and Alienor strode forth with courageous ease.

PART 7—WAR

Upon passing through the gateway that joined the many realms,
The battalion instantly was met with a wasteland of dead elms.
And as they all walked further through the twisted, charred remains,
They saw the castle set on high, above the desolate plains.

Cauchemar's words rippled through the company about,
His rage and courage ringing clear to those who heard his shout.
"This is the place where Deamhan staked his claim before,
And by power of all gathered here, it will happen no more."

Cauchemar walked forward with Alienor by his side
And knelt down at the same place where his family had died.
Taking up a handful of the cursed dirt closed in his fist,
He blew it from his palm and changed it into a green mist.

The mist formed a high wall, encircling all who had come to fight,
As Cauchemar in a loud voice called to Deamhan the White:
"Deamhan, come forth and look upon the face you so fear!
And see the great host Alienor has brought with her here!"

Cauchemar's voice echoed like vengeful, pealing thunder,
Clearing the dead elms and breaking high stone walls asunder.
From the turrets of the castle came a great black horde of crows,
Darkening the sky like a blanket of wicked, shrieking woes.

Alienor walked forward with her hand raised to the sky
And to the wicked horde let out a commanding cry:
"Turn you away from here, you wicked fowl of this land!
You are released from Deamhan's grip by the power of my hand!"

At once the flock dispersed with a sound like shattered glass;
To the four corners of the sky went the black birds wheeling pass.
Alienor gave no smile, but looked toward Deamhan's hall,
Knowing that the sorcerer could not but heed her call.

Dark clouds formed then overhead, and soon a rain heavily fell,
And from the black tower came the low sound of a bell
Tolling deep and loud to make the ground shiver and break,
And before the host convened, from the earth did the dead wake.

Deamhan's army of the dead rose clad in black woven mail
And charged in force at the invaders to strike and assail.
Cauchemar then cast forth the green mist he had conjured,
Sending the first back to the grave from which they had wandered.

Forêt cried aloud and pointed with his gleaming elven sword,
And to his soldiers these words from his heart then poured:
"Fight now for your homes, and fight now to end the next war!
Fight for peaceful life! For Cauchemar, for Alienor!"

At his words, the host then gave a great, united shout,
And the armies of elves and faeries rushed bravely out
To meet the dead of Deamhan with a thunderous clash
As spell-forged weapons turned the host of bone and mail to ash.

But the dead army was quick and had greater strength hidden yet,
And soon fell many mighty warriors of Titania and Forêt.
But Cauchemar charged on and with bare hands tore through the damned,
And tall and fierce upon the mount of ash did he then stand.

He turned to see Alienor nearby, doing just the same,
Smiting Deamhan's dead army with neither fear nor shame,
Her long sword shimmering in what little light was to be found
As she struck with violent force the demons rising from the ground.

Titania strode forth through the clearing made by them there
And raised high her arms into the battle-choked air.
And from the dry, dead earth did righteous, new life break through
As thrashing vines sprang from the ash and the dead army slew.

Grasping at the heels and binding Deamhan's dead forces,
The elves and faeries charged forth like vengeful war horses.
As they neared the castle gates, lightning struck at their feet,
And there before them all, Deamhan the White stood to meet.

As the armies held their ranks, the leaders sallied forth
To face the one who threatened as far as south is from north.
Forêt, Titania, Cauchemar, and brave young Alienor
Stood fast to end Deamhan and his vile reign forevermore.

Deamhan clenched his white fists in obvious wrath and rage,
Prepared to show these fools the true power of a mage.
But Alienor called out before any could be shown
And made the fierce resolve of all standing clearly known.

"Stay your hand, dark sorcerer, and your crafts so vile,
For your power is rooted in naught but deceit and guile.
We stand before you now absent of fear in our hearts,
For your tyrannical rule does from this day depart!"

In swift accord, the queen, the elf, and the girl rushed on,
Each there determined to bring down the wicked Deamhan.
Cauchemar cried out to stop them in their courageous haste,
For he knew the true tricks of Deamhan had not yet been faced.

Deamhan smiled as the heroes rushed forth to where he stood,
For in so doing, they did precisely what he had hoped they would.
Deamhan snapped his long and gnarled fingers as they ran,
And so, set them in the iron grips of his nefarious plan.

The black mist of Cauchemar's fears rose and bound his friends,
But 'twas not fear that sparked in him at Deamhan's possible ends.
For Cauchemar's eyes had lost of their color of emerald green—
As he then spoke to Deamhan, vivid red was all that was seen.

Cauchemar appeared taller as he came storming toward his foe.
With each deep-seated breath, his horns and claws did longer grow.
"Release them, I command, Deamhan, and face me now alone,
For you shall now see power and magic of this realm not yet known.

"You took from me all that I loved in my harmonious life:
My tribe, my race, my home, even my children and wife!
Now you shall know what exists beneath this peaceful shell.
Now you shall feel the wrath of all who by your hand have fell!"

Cauchemar's scaled flesh began to transform as he spoke,
And all watched in full wonder as the beast within him woke.
The black mist upon the three allies faded in Deamhan's new fear,
For all there in awe bore witness as a dragon did appear.

PART 8—THE BRAVE GIRL, THE QUEEN, THE ELF, THE SORCERER, AND THE DRAGON

Forêt, Titania, and Alienor found themselves released
As the cackling of Deamhan was by this new turn ceased.
Cauchemar towered over the wicked mage and spoke:
"You see now the terrible wrath you kindled and woke.

"For too long have I fled from you far and wide in tremulous fear,
But Cauchemar's flight shall end now and end right here.
You will be shown no mercy and given here no quarter.
All to be left of your name will be but dust and mortar!

"Forêt, Titania, Alienor, now get behind me please,
For I shall render Deamhan as blackened as the trees.
The fire of Cauchemar shall burn with vengeful heat
As I remind this fool that he is no more than meat!"

Cauchemar reared back and beat his wings against the wind
And breathed a fire that would bring even hard stone to an end.
Deamhan raised high his hands, conjuring a shield of mist,
As the two forces struck with all the might of a god's fist.

Cauchemar pushed harder to consume Deamhan with flame,
And Deamhan blocked his fire, to be pushed back all the same.
His feet had left deep tracks, as this was more than he could bear.
Forêt and Titania moved quick to end Deamhan then and there.

But of Deamhan's power they still were not wary enough.
As they neared the sorcerer, thorns he called forth to rebuff.
Trapped they were then in a cage of sharp, constricting briars
As Deamhan's power began to gain traction amidst the fires.

Deamhan pushed back more and smiled a wicked, vile grin,
Certain he would be the victor of these grounds again.
But as he sought destruction, as his pride grew more and more,
He failed to count the power of the mighty Alienor.

For with a motion fluid as a steady woodland stream,
She walked straight through the fire and conjurer's steam.
Looking Deamhan in his eye as she broke through his shield,
She drew forth the enchanted sword she was destined to wield.

"Deamhan, oh Deamhan, how little you still understand.
No matter your power, you'll breathe no more on this land.
Titania and Forêt fight so that their realm shall not end,
But I, Alienor, fight only out of love for my dear friend.

"So stand there and struggle to hold off the burning flame
While I tell you one final time your destroyer's name."
As she spoke these words, she held the sword high overhead,
Poised and ready to make certain Deamhan lay dead.

"You displayed your power only to bask in wicked pride,
Laughing as you walked upon the bones of those who died.
But by my sword, I swear now, you shall bring death no more.
And by my sword you will now know that I am Alienor!"

As she spoke her words, she swung the blade of ancient spell,
And Deamhan's vile, conjuring hands from his wrists then fell.
Titania and Forêt were released from their thorny cage
And rushed forth to then also pierce this most evil mage.

Titania threw her vines and bound him by his throat and arms
As Forêt with his sword struck true, ending all of Deamhan's charms.
Cauchemar's flame was focused on the sorcerer's eyes,
And, for a time, the only sound was Deamhan's anguished cries.

As the fire flew into the foe's bound flesh to therein burn,
A black and gray color Deamhan's shattered skin did turn.
The three allies stood back as Cauchemar took a deep, long breath
And with a final burst of flame, cemented Deamhan's death.

PART 9—DEPARTING FROM PALAIS DES RÊVES

As the smoke rose from the ashes of their vanquished foe,
Cauchemar took flight, and into the wind did he go.
His mighty wings beat the air, sending the clouds away,
And let the sun to shine bright upon this victorious day.

As he landed, he returned once more to his familiar shape
And took a moment to take in the battle-worn landscape.
"Friends, come near, for we cannot leave this place as it stands.
With your help, we can now restore these once lush lands.

"Join me, please, for we together can see this task done,
For magic is never greater than when it's cast as one.
All of our success has come from Alienor's brave hand,
And she will be the vessel to which we restore this land."

The three then gathered 'round, with Alienor at their center,
And as they joined hands, light from all around came to enter.
Alienor knelt down and placed her crown of laurels on the ground,
And the light poured through the laurels and gave a mighty sound.

The sound was not as thunder or like the crack of timber,
But the very ground seemed to laugh and leap, nimble and limber.
From its joyous bounding sprang new life as far as could be seen
As the crown of laurels summoned forth all that should be green.

The party then released their hands and, gazing all about,
Were filled with delight at the new landscape that did sprout.
What once stood as an evil mark of torment and of death
Now seemed to sing aloud with bright, reincarnated breath.

Titania spoke first, as her duty was as queen:
"Blessed is this land that by our hands has been made clean,
Restored now to its time before the evil one's dread mark.
And now has come time we must to our own realm embark."

Cauchemar spoke next to all, as was his rightful place,
Speaking as a king to Titania and Forêt's face:
"Indeed, you must return, but my true place belongs here,
For Deamhan's magic runs deep, and I must keep it clear.

"I sense that life is not all lost here upon this plane.
I will seek out the survivors so a new life I may gain."
Cauchemar then went to where the laurel crown still lay
And made of it four pieces in a hallowed display.

"A piece for Forêt to carry back to the elven land,
And with it he may call upon me should he need my hand.
A piece for Titania to hold within the hidden cave
As a reminder to all who see it of the life she did save.

"And last, a piece for you, brave Alienor, to keep near
So that you may come whenever you wish to be here.
For in Palais des Rêves, you are truly royal.
No one is more worthy to stand upon this soil.

"Simply hold the laurel and speak our names aloud,
And we shall come to aid you, no matter the quest or crowd.
For we are liberators of all victims of pain,
And we shall ensure they all receive their due gain!"

The Song of Circe and Other Simple Musings

As he spoke these words, a new veil was lifted from here,
And the place of the beginning was seen bright and clear.
Forêt and Titania passed through with no parting word,
And soon there was not a sound to be anywhere heard.

Cauchemar turned away to begin his search about the land
When something gently took his clawed and scaly hand.
And to his delight, he saw that Alienor had not departed.
Alienor spoke to Cauchemar as his tears flowing started:

"I've no need for laurels if I wish to see your face,
For here in this green land with you is my only true place.
I've naught to return to in the land from which I came,
So I'd rather stay here with you, if it's all the same."

So Palais des Rêves was now the home of these two,
And they walked forth in peace as the new forest fully grew.
A resurrected king and bravest of any queen,
Because she saw past the monster all others would have seen.

ABOUT THE AUTHOR

Born and raised in Richmond, VA, J. Matthew Helms is a husband, a father of two sons, and a project manager with a custom construction company. He has also been a writer of poetry for as long as he can recall. He believes in the stories that can be told, the imagery that can be conveyed, and how each one is inherently tailored to the mind's eye of the reader.

While poetry has been a part of his self-expression for many years, it became a lifeline just over seven years ago when he made the choice to become sober. His poetry often reflects the wide range of emotions that come from battling addiction. Many others are inspired by his best friend and companion, his wife of nearly twenty years.

When not writing, working, or spending time with his family, he can often be found wandering Richmond with a camera in his hand. His photography has been featured in a number of local shows and galleries.

www.ingramcontent.com/pod-product-compliance
Lightning Source LLC
LaVergne TN
LVHW011421080426
835512LV00005B/189